HOW I GOT MY KNEES BROWN

1st Edition

Published in 2011 by
Woodfield Publishing Ltd
Bognor Regis PO21 5EL England
www.woodfieldpublishing.co.uk

Copyright © 2011 Rupert C. Extence

All rights reserved

This publication is protected by international law. No part of its contents may be copied, reproduced or transmitted in any form or by any means, electronic or mechanical, or be stored in any information storage & retrieval system, without prior permission in writing from Woodfield Publishing Ltd

The right of Rupert C. Extence to be identified as author of this work has been asserted in accordance with the Copyright, Designs and Patents Act 1988

ISBN 1-84683-134-2

Printed and bound in England

Cover design by Nicolai Pastorius

How I Got My Knees Brown

The Overseas Experiences of an Erk (RAF Serviceman) from Devonshire during World War Two

Rupert C. Extence

Woodfield

Woodfield Publishing Ltd
Bognor Regis ~ West Sussex ~ England ~ PO21 5EL
tel 01243 821234 ~ **e/m** info@woodfieldpublishing.co.uk

Interesting and informative books on a variety of subjects

For full details of all our published titles, visit our website at
www.woodfieldpublishing.co.uk

To Miriam, who wrote to me every one of the 214 weeks that I was away, giving me something to look forward to when the post arrived, who was there to meet me off the train when I got home, and who helped me adjust to normal life again.

And above all to Mary, the girl who married me on 22nd January 1949 and has supported me through thick and thin ever since.

~ CONTENTS ~

Acknowledgements v

Foreword ix

Introduction xi

1. UK Service 1
   A sign in the sky 1
   Signing on 1
   Preparing for war 3
   Opening shots 3
   The London Blitz 3
   No.8 ITW Newquay 4
   The war comes to Shaldon 5
   Wartime train travel 6

2. Overseas Service 9
   Leaving Devon 9
   Wilmslow transit camp 9
   The SS Strathmore 11
   In convoy 11
   A Cape Town welcome 13
   Rounding the Cape 15
   A first look at Aden 16
   Port Tewfick 16
   By train to Beirut 18
   263 Wing Headquarters, Beirut 19
   A spell in hospital 23
   A traitor in our midst 25
   A chat with the general 25
   A high standard of nimbleness 26
   King's Regulations 28
   18 Sector Operations Room, RAF Gaza 29
   The battle of Alamein 33

Christmas in Gaza, 1942	34
A parade to remember	35
An angel of mercy	36
A good pair of boots	37
Netanya	38
Fallen comrades	39
Air Headquarters Levant, Jerusalem	40
The intelligence section	42
Information gathering	44
A well-intentioned deception	44
Learning to speak German	45
A historic opportunity	45
An interrupted train journey	47
The Dead Sea	48
All good things...	49
Posted to Syria	50
An uncomfortable plane ride	50
Advanced Air Headquarters, Aleppo	51
Spartan conditions	51
Christmas in Syria, 1943	54
My 21st birthday, Aleppo 1944	56
Operation Saturn	57
An amazing coincidence	58
A night out in Beirut	59
120 Maintenance Unit, Ras el Ain, Palestine	60
Guarding the perimeter	62
A shot in the dark	63
The sound of gunfire	64
Beer and a singsong	65
A promotion of sorts	66
The WAAF arrive	66
Moving on again	67
Air Headquarters, Aden	69
Too darn hot	70
The accommodation	71
The food	72
Recreation	72
Something to send home	73

	Still work to be done...	74
	Promotion and a lucky escape	75
	Funeral duty	75
	Christmas in Aden, 1944	77
	VE Day	78
	I stand in for the warrant officer	78
	The end of hostilities	80
	Waiting to go home	81
3.	**The Long Journey Home**	**83**
	By plane to Cairo	83
	Troopship to Marseilles	85
	Slow Train to Dieppe	87
	Circling Paris	90
	Ferry to Newhaven	91
	A final scare	91
	England at last	92
	Dispersal Camp	93
	By train to Devon and home	94

List of Illustrations

Greetings message from the CO. 2
List of 56th Entry Apprentices. 2
Troopship newsletter for the amusement of all on board. 12
The delights of Cape Town. 14
Watching the match at Beirut football stadium 1942. 22
Visit of Army 'top brass' to 263 Fighter Wing HQ Beirut, 1941. 26
Services pals on Beirut beach, 1941. 28
18 Sector Operations Room staff, RAF Gaza, winter 1942/43. 30
The camp cinema (after a gale), RAF Gaza, 1942. 32
Army Field Hospital at Rafah, Sinai Desert, February 1942/3 37
The author, wearing hospital 'blues' suit, February 1943 38
Notre Dame Convent Jerusalem 1943. 41
The Author standing beside the United Nations Guard Room, 1993.... 42
Former Air Headquarters Building in 1993. 43
Air HQ Levant staff outing to the Dead Sea, 1943. 48
Floating in the Dead Sea, 1943. 49
Advanced Air Headquarters Staff, Christmas 1943, Syria...................... 55
Spitfire Day, Aleppo 1944 – to raise funds to build new planes. 55
My permanent pass for the year 1944 at Advanced Air HQ. 56
Cutting from the Shaldon local paper. 59
Walter Stoneman, 120 Maintenance Unit. Palestine, 1944. 61
Headquarters Aden Command staff, 1945. 70
Brown knees & pith helmets, Aden 1944. 71
Swimming at steamer point, Aden, 1944. 73
A modern-day view of Shaldon. 95
The Author, with Service Medals, 2012. 98

Preface

This book came about more by accident than design. In 2009 the Western Morning News was asking for reminiscences of the First two years of the Second World War. I submitted an item and, as an afterthought sent a copy to my old school, by then Teignmouth Community College. It was used for the first time in 2010 and I received a lovely, home made, "Thank You" card signed by all 111 pupils and staff of Year 9. That inspired me to write the full story, which has proved to b quite a therapeutic experience.

Acknowledgements

To my daughter Andrea for all her support by way of encouragement and typing up the manuscript. Also to Year 9 (2010) Students at Teignmouth Community College whose enthusiastic reception of my story of the early part of my RAF service encouraged me to carry on and write the remaining wartime experience.

Foreword

Just a lad of 16 when he joined the RAF in 1939, young Rupert Extence could have had little idea of what the next six years held in store for him. They were to take him far from his home village of Shaldon near Teignmouth in picturesque Devonshire to the very different climate of the Middle East, where he would attempt to ply his newly-acquired administrative skills in what can only be described as 'adverse conditions'.

His descriptions of his experiences are delivered with a wonderfully dry Devonian sense of humour, as he relives the many difficulties and discomforts of his wartime existence and recalls how he and his colleagues rose to the challenge of performing their allocated duties in spite of the many shortcomings of their working conditions.

His reminiscences draw attention to the vital work provided by military administrative staff during the wartime years, without whose efforts the enormous logistical task of transporting, supplying and tending to the countless practical needs of the hundreds of thousands of military personnel serving at the time would not have been possible.

Introduction

Length of service is considered of great importance in the RAF and bragging rights inevitably go to those who have served the longest.

Anyone who has served in the Royal Air Force will be familiar with the phrase "Get your knees brown!"

Usually delivered by a Corporal or Sergeant with many years of experience under his belt to an inexperienced recruit or 'sprog', it is an invitation to gain some experience or "get some in" (another popular expression peculiar to the RAF).

The brown knees, of course, can only be achieved by undertaking a tour of duty overseas in one of the more far-flung RAF outposts, where short trousers are the regulation attire.

1. UK Service

In 1939 I was 16, living in Shaldon in Devonshire and in my last year at Teignmouth Grammar school. Despite Neville Chamberlain's "Peace in our Time" efforts, preparations for war were going ahead. Air raid shelters were being dug into the school sports field and Hitler's ranting speeches could be heard on the radio.

A sign in the sky

At the beginning of the year, we had been treated to a magnificent display of "The Northern Lights" over Dartmoor, a very unusual event at such a southerly latitude. According to some, this was a portent of war.

Signing on

I left school on 28th July. Three days later, I attended the selection process for an apprenticeship with the Royal Air Force. On the 1st August I signed a contract that would tie me to that Service until I was past 30 years of age.

Greetings from the C.O.

"In the very short time that I have been in command of the Record Office, I naturally have not had the fullest opportunity of acquainting myself with the many phases of the Apprentices' training here. I do, however, feel that what little I have seen of this training is sound and of tremendous benefit to you Apprentices.

Whilst you may lack some of the amenities enjoyed by Apprentices at Halton and Cranwell, there is no reason to regard your period of training here as dull and monotonous. By displaying keenness, initiative and a willingness to repay the Service for granting you one of the finest opportunities that confront the youth of to-day, you can make your few months here happy ones and of decided value both to yourself and the Service.

This small magazine offers you a medium for expression. Its pages are your own preserve. They fill one of the many gaps in your Unit life, so do make the fullest use of them.

Whilst wishing the magazine a very successful future, I realise that such success is entirely dependent upon the enthusiasm and co-operation of the Apprentices.

D. HARRIES,
Air Commodore.

Ruislip.
16.8.39.

Greetings message from the CO.

Greetings to the 56th Entry, and best wishes for a profitable and happy eighteen months.

591766 Almond, J.	591785 Hadfield, L.	591807 Pelluet, N. A.
767 Beckett, J. H.	787 Harrison, R. W.	808 Ralph, R.
761 Begg, W.	789 Hogben, S. J.	810 Smith, J. T.
760 Brow, A. L.	790 James, E. J.	813 Stowers-Hull, A.
776 Chapple, D. C.	769 Johnston, J.	814 Teague, W. K.
781 Constantine, K.	791 Kay, A. F.	820 Tombs, W. E.
771 Davies, J.	795 Langridge, J.	823 Young, C. E. W.
775 Elliott, R.	798 Liddell, G. K. H.	821 Weighell, R.
782 Extence, R. C.	763 Mackay, J. M.	824 Whatley, W. G.
779 Fletcher, H. T.	804 Marshall, P.	822 Wilcox, T. F.
788 Gawthorpe, H.	828 Marshall, S. N.	829 Williams, D. T. R.
784 Grindey, J. H.	806 Morgan, V. G.	805 Parker, V. C.
772 Ashwood, E. G.	803 Neville, A. W.	812 Pirret, R.
773 Beddoe, E.	759 Hogg, J.	765 Scott, J. E.
780 Bennett, J. E.	762 Jackson, W. C.	811 Southwell, D. W.
768 Burrows, W.	794 Johnson, J.	815 Sutherland, R.
770 Connor, E. L.	792 Jones, B.	816 Thompson, R. G.
802 Cumiskey, G.	793 Lane, J. L.	817 Tozer, L. R.
774 Doyle, J. B.	830 Ledingham, A. P.	818 Warwick, V. C.
777 Evans, A. E.	796 Lyons, T. L.	819 Wellington, R.
778 Fairley, R. V.	797 Malkin, J. B.	826 Whitelaw, P. D.
783 Gammage, E. W. J.	799 Marshall, J. F.	825 Wilks, J. H.
786 Graham, C. T.	801 Matthews, D. F.	827 Willis, E. R.
	809 Murphy, T. F.	
	764 Nicholson, G.	

List of 56th Entry Apprentices.

2 ~ How I Got My Knees Brown

Preparing for war

Whilst "square bashing" that month at the Apprentice School in North London, we saw the BOAC airliners being flown north from Croydon Airport to less vulnerable areas. All RAF Reserve airmen were mobilised. The call-up letters had long been prepared and were stored with each individual's service documents for all the various mobilisation centres across the country. Our senior apprentices were used to man those centres, dropping off the call-up letters to the Post Office and then travelling on with the documents. Only three weeks into my career I was involved in this exercise – helping to load the three-ton lorries used!

Opening shots

My first taste of action was on Shaldon Bridge. It was a beautiful summer evening in August 1940. I was walking over the bridge when I heard the sound of anti-aircraft gunfire and bomb explosions. Newton Abbot Railway station was being attacked and I could see the enemy aircraft involved. As I watched, they turned and flew very low over the river, heading seaward, hotly pursued by two RAF Hurricanes with all guns blazing. Needless to say, I flattened myself in the gutter.

The London Blitz

Soon afterwards I returned to my RAF Station and the London Docklands Blitz began. Then followed six weeks of nights spent in air raid shelters, listening to gunfire and bombs, with the occasional 'stick' being dropped near enough to hear the whistle as they fell. By night the sky to the south-east was red with fires while by day the Battle of Britain (as it would later be called) raged.

No.8 ITW Newquay

By mid-October I had finished my training and joined the 20-strong party setting up No.8 Initial Training Wing (ITW) at the Trebarwith Hotel in Newquay. To my consternation the personnel included Warrant Officer "Percy" Parkes. I had just endured fifteen months of his ministrations as our Station Warrant Officer at the apprentice school. Five foot nothing, a voice like a foghorn and a strict disciplinarian, I think he invented the concept of 'zero tolerance'! He met us at the railway station on our arrival for the selection process, and personally taught us drill and every aspect of smartness, as well as inspecting us every morning on parade and our huts for cleanliness and tidiness, including our beds and kit layout. He had been carrying out these duties for years and must have been known, and feared, by every apprentice who had been subjected to his tender ministrations. It was inconceivable that he would ever be moved and yet, here he was, in Newquay! What had I done to deserve this fate?

I need not have worried. He treated me as if I was his own son, told everyone who cared to listen that I was a product of his training and would have no one else to act as escort to those appearing before the Commanding Officer each morning charged with various offences. He justified this on the grounds that I was the only airman on the Wing who could march properly and that was only because he had taught me!

Once the Wing was up and running, part of my job was issuing travel warrants, rail journey itineraries, leave passes and ration cards for staff and also for the 200 trainees each week completing their ground training and moving on to Flying Training Schools. On alternate weeks, all 200 would go either to Liverpool or Glasgow to join troopships taking them to Canada, South Africa or Rhodesia after being given embarkation leave. For these I had to arrange transport with the railway company (GWR) and liaise with the Wing Warrant Officer for an escort party and the Cookhouse for travel rations. On at least one occasion I had to recall all 200 from leave, which meant dictating that many names and addresses over the telephone. The girl at the Post Office taking the telegram details was probably about the same age as myself. I doubt if 17-year-olds would be given that level of responsibility today.

The war comes to Shaldon

By this time, coming home on leave was like going to the Front Line. There was barbed wire all along the sea and river fronts, tank traps on the beaches, Naval guns on the Ness, anti-aircraft guns and machine gun positions all around and sentries posted on each side of the river to guard the Shaldon Bridge approach roads. In addition to the inevitable blackout, nothing was allowed on the river during the hours of darkness and the drawbridge section of the bridge was raised between midnight and 6am, cutting Shaldon off completely. If your train was badly delayed, it would mean leaving it at Newton Abbot and walking the five miles from there.

Wartime train travel

At times travelling between Newquay and Teignmouth meant running the gauntlet of the Plymouth Blitz. On one occasion when I was travelling homeward, the train was stopped between Keyham and Devonport. With all the anti-aircraft batteries and Naval ships firing and bombs and incendiaries dropping, it was an inferno but, remarkably, I fell asleep!

The previous night I had been on duty on our telephone exchange, taking messages about air raid warnings, so had worked for almost 36 hours straight, except for meal breaks. I woke to find myself being shaken and told to get off the train as the line had been hit ahead of us. We were transferred by buses to Plymouth North Road station. A previous train that I had just missed at Par was there, severely damaged by incendiary bombs.

The second occasion was less traumatic. I was on the way back to Cornwall when we were stopped at Plympton station. It was a beautiful, clear, frosty night with a full moon. I and most of the other passengers got out on the platform and were watching the mayhem in progress over Plymouth when, suddenly, there was the tell-tale whistle of a stick of bombs descending. I dived under a platform seat in a flash! Every time I went through Plympton after that, I would look for that seat and remember the moment.

On another occasion the situation in Plymouth was so bad we were diverted all around by the old Southern Railway branch lines in North Cornwall and North Devon. What a weird experience that was!

First of all there was the blackout, then there was the fact that all station nameplates and any other identifying signs had long since been removed in case of invasion and, on top of that, there were no announcements whatsoever. Luckily, my knowledge of the railway system was sufficient for me to know that we should reach Exeter St Davids at some time.

The train was packed like the proverbial tin of sardines and I was squatting on my kitbag in a carriage corridor. Every time we stopped, which was frequently, I would peer out into the darkness in the vain hope of recognising where we were. The only large station at which we stopped was Okehampton and I almost got out there by mistake.

Eventually we reached Exeter, where we were greeted by a porter shouting the station name! It was 5 am whereas I would normally have reached Teignmouth at 8pm the previous evening. Never mind, I was in good time to catch the first train down and I had avoided being stranded in Teignmouth until Shaldon Bridge reopened!

In my view our railway men and women were the unsung heroes of the Home Front. Despite constant disruption and danger, they responded to every demand to move large numbers of troops, their equipment and supplies, often at very short notice, while maintaining a viable service for civilian passengers and goods. The road network in those days could never have coped with the demand.

And so into 1941 when, on my 18th birthday, I could remove my light blue cap band and apprentice badge and become a fully-fledged aircraftsman.

Not many months later I was on my way to Glasgow myself, to join a troopship bound for Egypt on a deployment that would last for 4 years and 6 weeks.

2. Overseas Service

A signal received by RAF St Eval was awaiting collection. After another routine trip with our driver I handed it over to our Sergeant. He opened it, read it, and said, "you are on your way abroad son." I had to report to RAF Wilmslow at the beginning of August. Time was so short I could only have 48 hours embarkation leave instead of the usual 14 days. I had spent the last seven months arranging the travel and paperwork for hundreds of trainee aircrew who were going to various overseas destinations for their flying training. Now I was doing the same for myself.

Leaving Devon

I left Newquay on the same train I normally used when going on a weekend pass to my home in Teignmouth. It connected at Par with an overnight Penzance-Manchester train. This time there were no air raids at Plymouth to delay us. What a strange feeling not to be getting out at Teignmouth. As we ran down the River Teign, along the coast and back up the Exe, I took a hard, long look. I had no idea when, or indeed if, I would see those views again.

Wilmslow transit camp

Next morning I arrived at the Wilmslow transit camp. Then followed two weeks confined to camp with no chance to go out and sample the delights of Wilmslow (if there were any). Days of massive inactivity interspersed with mundane matters like medical inspections, inoculations and kit issue. We received our khaki drill outfit, complete with a magnificent sun helmet, circa The Boer War. The draft ahead of us was issued with cold weather gear whilst the one behind us received tropical gear.

Only after the war did I discover that one was a Hurricane Squadron on its way to Russia whilst the other was bound for Singapore. I was relieved to know that I had missed those options!

The days at Wilmslow were mostly spent lying on our beds listening to Workers Playtime and current popular tunes such as 'Anapola' and 'Red Sails in the Sunset'. Even now if I hear them I am back there in the Transit Camp, wondering what the future held.

At last we were told we would be on the move that night and we marched to Wilmslow Station in the blackout at 1am. Presumably the thinking behind this was that enemy spies did not work unsociable hours.

Anyway, we entrained and rumbled off to where we knew not. It happened to be Glasgow Docks, which we reached later that same morning. Then, after much hanging about on the dockside, we were up the gangplank of the P&O liner "Strathmore" and ushered to what would be our home for the next six weeks.

The SS Strathmore

Twenty Mess tables accommodating 18 men each, located in a section of what previously had been a cargo hold, was to be the area in which we lived, ate and slept. When the weather allowed, we would be permitted to go up on deck and find enough space to get some fresh air.

Three times a day, two men from each table would collect food in buckets from the galley, which was at the other end of the ship. On the way to and fro we passed the Officers Dining Room, where tables were laid with all the finery associated with an Ocean Liner. Outside the doors the menu of the day was displayed, listing many courses and choices which we enviously read before sitting down to eat our plates of stew or boiled fish, although for most of us there would be times ahead when we would be glad of even that Spartan fare.

We sailed as dusk began to fall, going on deck to watch the Scottish coast and Western Isles slip past and fade from view. For most of us it would be the last we would see of our homeland for many years; and for some, ever.

In convoy

The next morning we were well out to sea. A sea filled with ships of all shapes and sizes as far as the eye could see. Merchant ships large and small, our accompanying troopships 'Strathnaver' and 'Orion' and our escorting warships, the command ship HMS 'Repulse' and various destroyers and frigates. Less than six months later the 'Repulse' was sunk by the Japanese near Singapore.

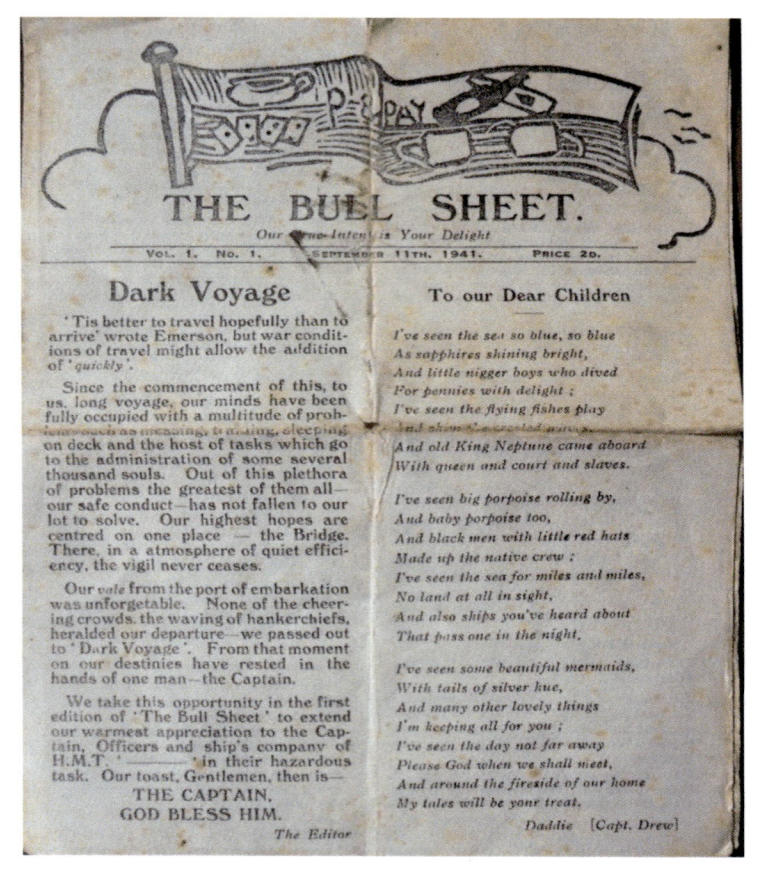

THE BULL SHEET.

Our ∞mo-Intent is Your Delight

VOL. 1.　NO. 1.　SEPTEMBER 11TH, 1941.　PRICE 2D.

Dark Voyage

'Tis better to travel hopefully than to arrive' wrote Emerson, but war conditions of travel might allow the addition of '*quickly*'.

Since the commencement of this, to us, long voyage, our minds have been fully occupied with a multitude of problems—such as messing, training, sleeping on deck and the host of tasks which go to the administration of some several thousand souls. Out of this plethora of problems the greatest of them all—our safe conduct—has not fallen to our lot to solve. Our highest hopes are centred on one place — the Bridge. There, in an atmosphere of quiet efficiency, the vigil never ceases.

Our vale from the port of embarkation was unforgetable. None of the cheering crowds, the waving of hankerchiefs, heralded our departure—we passed out to 'Dark Voyage'. From that moment on our destinies have rested in the hands of one man—the Captain.

We take this opportunity in the first edition of 'The Bull Sheet' to extend our warmest appreciation to the Captain, Officers and ship's company of H.M.T. _____ in their hazardous task. Our toast, Gentlemen, then is—

THE CAPTAIN,
GOD BLESS HIM.

The Editor

To our Dear Children

I've seen the sea so blue, so blue
As sapphires shining bright,
And little nigger boys who dived
For pennies with delight ;
I've seen the flying fishes play
And skim o'er crested waves.
And old King Neptune came aboard
With queen and court and slaves.

I've seen big porpoise rolling by,
And baby porpoise too,
And black men with little red hats
Made up the native crew ;
I've seen the sea for miles and miles,
No land at all in sight,
And also ships you've heard about
That pass one in the night.

I've seen some beautiful mermaids,
With tails of silver hue,
And many other lovely things
I'm keeping all for you ;
I've seen the day not far away
Please God when we shall meet,
And around the fireside of our home
My tales will be your treat.

Daddie [Capt. Drew]

Troopship newsletter for the amusement of all on board.

To make tracking by submarines difficult, every 15 minutes the whole convoy would change direction by 90 degrees. Even so, by taking the position of the sun, I calculated we

12 ~ *How I Got My Knees Brown*

were sailing westwards. Now and again, some of the escorting destroyers would leave their position and disappear into the distance, following which we would hear depth charges exploding.

For a while we must have been just out of sight of the American Coast, as you could smell the scents of land in the air. Then, after tracking back eastwards, we arrived at Freetown in West Africa.

For two days we experienced tropical heat, humidity and torrential rain. Everything was saturated. Matches were so damp it was almost impossible to light one to seek solace in a cigarette. My first experience of foreign shores – and I was not impressed!

We were glad to be at sea again, even though the submarines might be waiting for us. Off we sailed in another long loop until, early in September, we sighted land ahead. As it drew closer, we could make out the famous flat-topped shape of Table Mountain. Cape Town, South Africa – what bliss!

A Cape Town welcome

And what bliss indeed it was. Three days of shore leave, three pounds each in South African currency to spend, and, as we were soon to discover, the delightful experience of being treated like royalty. Never will I forget the warmth of our welcome. A queue of cars stretching from the dock gates waiting to take us for a day out around the Cape of Good

Hope, free forces canteens, shops refusing to take payment for cigarettes, sweets and chocolate; it became almost impossible to spend any money. On the third day my mates and I decided to delay going ashore until the waiting queue had gone. We spent the day being stopped by people asking us why we had not been picked up!

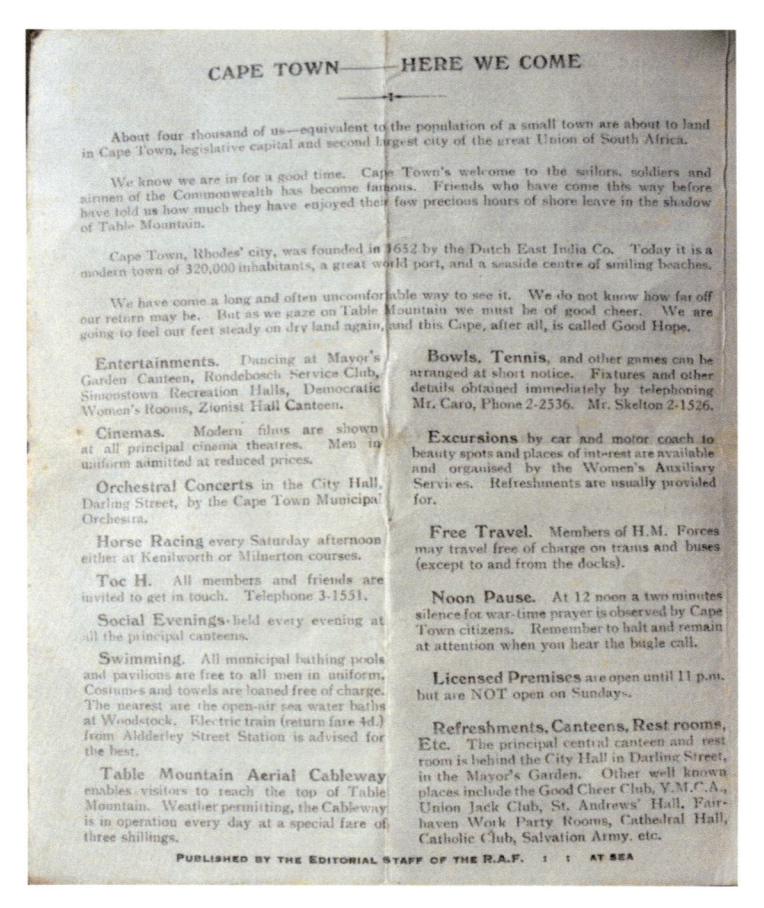

> ## CAPE TOWN —— HERE WE COME
>
> About four thousand of us—equivalent to the population of a small town are about to land in Cape Town, legislative capital and second largest city of the great Union of South Africa.
>
> We know we are in for a good time. Cape Town's welcome to the sailors, soldiers and airmen of the Commonwealth has become famous. Friends who have come this way before have told us how much they have enjoyed their few precious hours of shore leave in the shadow of Table Mountain.
>
> Cape Town, Rhodes' city, was founded in 1652 by the Dutch East India Co. Today it is a modern town of 320,000 inhabitants, a great world port, and a seaside centre of smiling beaches.
>
> We have come a long and often uncomfortable way to see it. We do not know how far off our return may be. But as we gaze on Table Mountain we must be of good cheer. We are going to feel our feet steady on dry land again, and this Cape, after all, is called Good Hope.
>
> **Entertainments.** Dancing at Mayor's Garden Canteen, Rondebosch Service Club, Simonstown Recreation Halls, Democratic Women's Rooms, Zionist Hall Canteen.
>
> **Cinemas.** Modern films are shown at all principal cinema theatres. Men in uniform admitted at reduced prices.
>
> **Orchestral Concerts** in the City Hall, Darling Street, by the Cape Town Municipal Orchestra.
>
> **Horse Racing** every Saturday afternoon either at Kenilworth or Milnerton courses.
>
> **Toc H.** All members and friends are invited to get in touch. Telephone 3-1551.
>
> **Social Evenings** held every evening at all the principal canteens.
>
> **Swimming.** All municipal bathing pools and pavilions are free to all men in uniform. Costumes and towels are loaned free of charge. The nearest are the open-air sea water baths at Woodstock. Electric train (return fare 4d.) from Aldderley Street Station is advised for the best.
>
> **Table Mountain Aerial Cableway** enables visitors to reach the top of Table Mountain. Weather permitting, the Cableway is in operation every day at a special fare of three shillings.
>
> **Bowls, Tennis,** and other games can be arranged at short notice. Fixtures and other details obtained immediately by telephoning Mr. Caro, Phone 2-2336. Mr. Skelton 2-1526.
>
> **Excursions** by car and motor coach to beauty spots and places of interest are available and organised by the Women's Auxiliary Services. Refreshments are usually provided for.
>
> **Free Travel.** Members of H.M. Forces may travel free of charge on trams and buses (except to and from the docks).
>
> **Noon Pause.** At 12 noon a two minutes silence for war-time prayer is observed by Cape Town citizens. Remember to halt and remain at attention when you hear the bugle call.
>
> **Licensed Premises** are open until 11 p.m. but are NOT open on Sundays.
>
> **Refreshments, Canteens, Rest rooms, Etc.** The principal central canteen and rest room is behind the City Hall in Darling Street, in the Mayor's Garden. Other well known places include the Good Cheer Club, Y.M.C.A., Union Jack Club, St. Andrews' Hall, Fairhaven Work Party Rooms, Cathedral Hall, Catholic Club, Salvation Army, etc.
>
> PUBLISHED BY THE EDITORIAL STAFF OF THE R.A.F. : : AT SEA

The delights of Cape Town.

Despite all the attention, we did manage to spend the day exploring Cape Town. By evening, still flush with practically all of our money, we decided on a meal in the poshest restaurant we could find, the "Del Monico" – drinks, relaxation in utter comfort and a fabulous meal of many courses. The cost? Five shillings each! On the way back to the Docks we purchased a sandbag filled with oranges, apples, etc for one shilling.

Rounding the Cape

During the night the convoy sailed and by morning we were rounding the Cape. For the next three days, that part of the ocean lived up to its reputation: howling gales, tumultuous seas, rolling, pitching and tossing endlessly.

Of the 18 lads on our Mess table, only two of us were not seasick for the whole time. It was a hazardous journey to and from the galley to collect food anyway. What a relief to reach calmer waters, when I could work out that we were sailing northwards.

The kindness and generosity of the people of Cape Town lived on not only in memory but also in ways that were more practical. They had donated enough additional supplies to enable us to enjoy much-enhanced menus on the remaining three Sundays of our voyage.

A first look at Aden

Our next port of call was Aden, that barren, rocky, hot and humid extinct volcano at the southern end of the Red Sea. Here we bade farewell to our Naval escort, as the submarine threat in the Red Sea had been eliminated earlier in the year. There were still many coal-fired ships in those days and it was fascinating to watch them being refuelled. A constant stream of coolies bearing baskets of coal on their heads were running down the jetty, tipping their load and then back again for more. A human conveyor belt!

The next day we sailed, singly now, for a quick three-day run up the Red Sea to Port Tewfik. Little did I know then that three years hence I would be sailing back down the Red Sea for a twelve-month spell in Aden.

Port Tewfick

Port Tewfick, gateway to the Mystic East! Well, to the sights, smells, heat and flies of the Canal Zone Egypt anyway. We disembarked, loaded our kit onto an open 3-ton army lorry, climbed aboard and were away up the desert road, the first of many such journeys. Our destination was Kasfareet transit camp. Butlins, it was not, just row upon row of small six-man tents, with not a stick of furniture of any kind. Here I was to experience another first, the art of sleeping on the ground with just a groundsheet and two blankets. Incidentally, the groundsheet was dual purpose; you used it as a cape when it rained. The Italian Prisoners of War in the camp next door had no such problems. Covered by the Geneva Convention, they enjoyed life in well-built wooden huts, no doubt well furnished with bunk beds, etc, and space aplenty for exercise, playing football or sunbathing. Their war was over, lucky devils.

How can I explain the delights of that transit camp? Two parades a day in the blistering sun, listening to endless lists of names of those who would be leaving next day to join their units; threats of an instant Court Martial if you missed your draft, the inevitable "gyppo tummy", food that made the troopship fare seem delicious and the demoralising daily task of 'tidying the desert' by collecting stones into neat piles. As there were no lights, these were usually scattered again in the night by people tripping over them.

After about 10 days of this routine, a great hue and cry went around the camp, ordering me to report to the Station Warrant Officer immediately. This I did, at top speed, filled with utmost trepidation. Not long afterwards I was ushered into his presence and standing stiffly to attention, as far as my trembling knees would allow.

"Where the **** have you been airman?" said he, in sternest tones. (I omit the expletives he used to save my readers' blushes)

"Nowhere, Sir," said I.

"Why did you not respond to your draft this morning?"

How I Got My Knees Brown ~ 17

"What draft?" said I, with visions of handcuffs and Military Prison flashing through my brain.

Once he had recovered his powers of speech, his next command followed at full volume.

"REPORT TO THE ORDERLY ROOM AT ONCE! AT THE DOUBLE, LEFT, RIGHT, LEFT, RIGHT..."

As you can imagine, I complied with all speed! After much shuffling and searching of papers the fellow airman attending to my needs told me that there seemed to have been a mistake (which in more modern times would be described as 'an administrative error'!) His officer, a young Pilot Officer then became involved. He took one look at my RAF service number and told me that he was an ex-apprentice himself and would sort things out.

Within 48 hours I was on my way to 263 Fighter Wing HQ rather than a Fighter Squadron in the Western Desert, which had been my intended destination. Wartime secrecy meant that you never knew where you were going until you got there!

By train to Beirut

About a dozen of us lads were given railway warrants and told to report to the RTO at Haifa. These knowledgeable gentlemen allegedly knew where all the various service units in their area were. In practice, they turned out to have little more than a vague idea of where they might be! Our travel instructions were to catch a train bound for Port Said, get off at El Kantara, take the ferry across the Suez Canal and catch the overnight train to Haifa. This trip provided three new experiences. Travelling for long distances on uncomfortable, hard, wooden-slatted seats; Middle Eastern style 'hole in the floor' toilets (requiring particular skill when attempting to use them aboard a swaying train); and travel rations consisting of bully beef sandwiches if you are lucky or hard tack biscuits if you were not.

Eventually we reached Haifa, at about 10am the next morning, and duly reported to the RTO. Luckily Geography was one of my favourite subjects at school, so I knew that we were in northern Palestine. The three of us bound for 263 Wing were put aboard a 3-ton truck about to leave for Beirut while the rest were told they would have to wait for transport going in their direction. Fortunately, the driver knew where 263 Wing was situated, which saved a lot of hassle at the other end.

The journey north along the coast road was beautiful, marred only by the evidence of the fighting that had taken place a couple of months earlier when Allied Forces had taken control of Syria and Lebanon from the Vichy French.

263 Wing Headquarters, Beirut

Eventually we reached our destination, a former French Foreign Legion barracks, and were soon shown around our new home, an empty barrack room devoid of all furniture other than a straw-filled pallaisse (mattress) each. This, I was to discover, was what I could expect everywhere I went, except for nine blissful months at Air Headquarters Levant in Jerusalem, where I enjoyed a regulation metal bed with standard "biscuit" style mattress and actual sheets! (Later on, in Aden, I was to endure a year on a wooden charpoy, complete with resident families of bed bugs. It was too hot to even think about any bedding.) All our kit and personal belongings would be stored in our kitbags, which could also double as a pillow.

The Foreign Legion barracks also boasted an interesting version of the 'hole in the floor' toilet. Instead of individual flush cisterns, all flushing came from one large tank located high in the ceiling. This emptied periodically, but fortunately not too frequently, every time the tank became full. The water came from a great height with considerable force. To avoid a drenching you had to listen carefully for the tank to stop filling and then leap out of the way the instant you heard the water begin to discharge.

Beirut was a beautiful city and very French in style and ambiance. Wing headquarters was situated in a large building in a spacious walled compound on the coast road between the port and airport. It had previously been the Vichy French Army HQ. The road had a wide promenade on the seaward side and was beautiful, with views of the mountain range behind Beirut to the north and the coastline to the south. On clear days you could see as far as the border with Palestine.

Our working hours were normally 8am to 1pm and 5pm to 8pm, six and a half days per week. That gave us a couple of hours to spend in the city centre. Transport was by taxi! These were old Fords with running boards. The usual loading, including those standing on the running boards, was 10! Cheap, but hazardous.

The worst bit was a fairly steep hill joined at the bottom on a blind corner by a tramline coming from the right. This was always taken at top speed and great was the relief when it was negotiated safely.

Talking of the Beirut trams, the drivers were very partial to our free issue "V for Victory" cigarettes, despite the fact that we considered them to be vile. We were allowed to travel free on the trams and I discovered that if I offered the driver one he would invariably allow me to drive the tram while he stood back and enjoyed a smoke! The best bit was working the foot pedal that changed the warning bell!

We were paid fortnightly, which gave me the magnificent sum of just over £2 to paint the town red but the exchange rate at the time converted that to well over 20 Lebanese pounds. Riches indeed for an Aircraftsman Second Class. Unfortunately, everything was that much dearer, which left you just as broke as ever in the second week of the pay cycle.

Watching the match at Beirut football stadium 1942.

There was one exception to this. On my way to work I passed a typical French-style bar with a barber's chair at one end. The barber was a young lad of my age called Feris Banadoora and we became quite good friends. He spoke four languages – Arabic, French, Italian and English – as all were taught in Lebanese schools at that time.

Anyway, for the equivalent of about one English penny a day he would give me a "cutthroat" razor shave, hot towels and all. The bar owner considered me to be such a regular customer he would treat me to a cherry brandy every Saturday! I do not remember ever seeing any other customers.

A spell in hospital

Sandfly Fever landed me in an Army Hospital for 48 hours. Two nights of bliss in a proper bed! The rest of the patients in the ward were all Australian soldiers. The 7th Australian Division had played a large part in the recent campaign against the Vichy French. One night the air raid sirens went and all the Aussies were under their beds in a flash and imploring me to follow suit. The fact that I didn't, much to their amazement, was not due to my having had much more experience of raids in the UK, but what could be called "insider knowledge".

I knew that it was no more than our weekly visit from a German reconnaissance aircraft or "shufti kite" in common parlance. This would be left to go on its way unmolested for two reasons. Firstly, it would be stripped of all non-essentials and flying far too high for any aircraft armed with guns to reach it. Secondly, we had no aircraft available anyway. Provided the necessary ground facilities were in place, the operational aircraft required could be moved in at very short notice.

Actually, the weekly visits did us a favour, as they provided an opportunity for our air defence systems, such as the operations room, aircraft tracking facilities, anti-aircraft gun and searchlight batteries, to practice their skills. For a while this air raid rehearsal was supplemented by the use of an ex-Vichy French biplane, which would take off and fly around for an hour or two.

Sadly, we lost the use of it when it crashed one night. As it happened, I was on duty that evening and remember letting the police Corporal from our perimeter gate past into the Operations Room. He marched in and smartly saluted the Officer of the watch, only to be told, "Just a minute Corporal, we have a flap on."

What the officer didn't mention was that the "flap" was because they had lost track of the aircraft. After about 15 minutes, the Officer said, "Well Corporal, what is it?"

"An aircraft has crashed through the perimeter fence Sir," came the reply!

After my short spell in hospital, I was sent to an Australian Convalescent camp high in the mountains behind Beirut for a week. My strongest memory of this was actually the drive up there on a narrow road with countless hairpin bends and fantastic views. Every road sign along the way seemed to have been used for target practice by various tanks or armoured cars that had passed by during earlier military operations. For seven whole days I was allowed to luxuriate in beautiful surroundings with plenty of good food and nothing to do all day except sit in the sun and dream of home.

Then it was back to reality and my Foreign Legion home. The only compensation was that I was not actually serving in the French Foreign legion itself!

A traitor in our midst

Life in 263 Wing had its moments. One such was when we caught a German spy. He was wearing the uniform of an RAF Sergeant and was actually English, although working for the Germans. He had been talking to some of our lads in town and his questions had made them suspicious.

The RAF Police had brought him in for questioning. I was on duty at HQ that evening and was given his pay book to examine. It was a bit scruffy and smudged, but otherwise seemed in order.

Looking at him across the room, it suddenly dawned on me that his Sergeant's chevrons were on the wrong arm of his jacket. [At that time an economy measure meant that they were only worn on one arm, and it was not the one he was using.] That misdemeanour was enough to put him under arrest for further examination. Eventually he was Court Martialled, found guilty, and had an early morning appointment with the Firing Squad.

A chat with the general

On another occasion when I was on duty at Headquarters we were visited by General Maitland Wilson, the then commander of British Forces in Palestine and Transjordan. He stopped and had a brief chat with me, a mere Aircraftsman Second Class and a "Brylcreem Boy" [as we were called by the army] to boot.

Visit of Army 'top brass' to 263 Fighter Wing HQ Beirut, 1941.

A high standard of nimbleness

On the 18th of June 1941, Winston Churchill issued instructions to the Chief of Air Staff that all ground personnel should be trained to a high standard of nimbleness and efficiency in the defence of their locations. Presumably in pursuance of this edict, we were given shooting practice on a nearby rifle range. Two of us in turn were detailed to man the targets. This entailed sheltering in a trench until firing had ceased, then recording the hits achieved and sticking paper patches over the bullet holes before raising the targets for the next would-be marksman to take pot-shots at. The signal that it was all clear to begin this process was given by an officer positioned some way behind the firing line and conveyed via field telephone.

One afternoon, when I was on target duty, the telephone was not working properly so the Officer in charge of the operation decided that we would use the bell signal alone. All went well for a couple of sessions but when the bell went again and I dutifully clambered out of the trench to the nearest target, a shot rang out and hit the target uncomfortably close to me.

I am sure that I exceeded Mr Churchill's required standard of 'nimbleness' in returning to the trench!

Apparently the erroneous ringing of the telephone had been caused by a passing Arab, who had spotted a box with a handle attached and decided to turn it to see what happened.

No doubt in today's jargon that would be classed as "friendly fire". One thing is certain, had we been required to follow modern Health and Safety regulations, with all the attendant 'risk assessments', we would never have been able to get out of bed, never mind get as far as the rifle range!

Another memorable moment was when a rather venerable three-engined Italian aircraft (CANT 1007 BIS) landed, literally out of the blue. Apparently its crew, after tiring of this warfare lark, had decided to surrender.

What happened to the aircraft I know not. An attempt to fly it inland to Damascus failed, as it was unable to reach the height required to fly over the mountain range inland.

Services pals on Beirut beach, 1941.

King's Regulations

Before leaving Beirut I must mention our Wing Headquarters copy of the Kings Regulations, which contained detailed instructions about how everything in the RAF should be done. As far as I can remember, it contained many procedures more applicable to the First World War, such as the wearing of puttees and stabling of horses. As a result, the venerable tome needed amending from time to time and the Adjutant had to sign inside the cover to confirm that the amendments had been made.

Imagine my amazement when, 10 years later, I was in the Canal Zone, Egypt, helping to set up a new NCO Training

School. I obtained a copy of "King's Regs" from Central Stores and found it to be the very same one.

18 Sector Operations Room, RAF Gaza

By the beginning of July 1942 the German breakthrough in the Western Desert had reached Alamein, and the Suez Canal, Egypt and Palestine were threatened. A year earlier the perceived threat had been from the north by way of a German attack through Turkey. This had led to the occupation of the Lebanon and Syria. 263 Wing had been formed to control the aerial defence of attacks from that quarter.

Now the threat was from the south, so to cover that direction, 18 Sector Operations Room was formed.

This involved about 30 of us, including myself, being packed on to two open-top 3-ton lorries and sent off to a destination known only to the officer in charge. The essential equipment I had been able to muster comprised one typewriter originally left behind by the Vichy French forces, one small and one larger wooden packing case. The typewriter went into the small case and that went into the large case, together with the personnel records and other necessary items. On arrival at our new location the larger case became a desk, the smaller one a chair and I was ready to produce Daily Routine Orders so that the war could continue.

Our journey took two days; first back down the beautiful coast road to the Palestine border, then through the fertile coastal plain and on to a much less fertile area, where we came to RAF Station Gaza, a pre-war airfield of wooden huts within a wire perimeter fence. However, there was no room for us, so we were directed to an empty Nissen hut a little way off, alongside the approach road. By comparison, our previous ex-Foreign Legion home was palatial. A rough concrete floor, breeze block walls that were home to a colony of bed bugs that hid themselves in the cracks and crannies and a corrugated iron roof that ensured excessive heat by day and cold by night. At least it kept the rain off! Our only lighting was a couple of paraffin oil lamps.

18 Sector Operations Room staff, RAF Gaza, winter 1942/43 (author in doorway).

Our operations room was set up in a single-storey building in the corner of an orange grove, about half a mile away, on the outskirts of Gaza itself. It was reached over open ground that still contained remnants of First World War trenches used in fighting against the Turkish Army.

Here we experienced another version of toilets, consisting of an open trench with a plank across it to perch upon, screened by hessian hung on a wooden framework. This screening vanished so frequently that we gave up replacing it and sat, or stood, as necessary, in full view of passers-by.

When we first arrived at Gaza, the airfield was the home of a squadron of dummy wooden Hurricane aircraft. After the weekly visit of the German 'shufty kite', these would be moved around to give the impression that they were in use. As ever, we used the opportunity to practice our aircraft tracking skills. Quite soon this all changed as the whole of the airfield was used as a testing and storage area for all types of fighter aircraft in preparation for the forthcoming offensive at Alamein. Ground crew worked in the blazing sunshine from dawn to dusk, seven days a week on this task. We also had three test pilots flight-testing the machines. Sadly, one of them lost his life in a crash, which I happened to witness.

The airfield was also used as a staging post for the weekly airmail flight from Cairo to RAF Ramleh, the nearest point for road transport to Air headquarters at Jerusalem. The return flight would stop and refuel at Gaza. The aircraft used was a very old and slow First World War bomber. An unfavourable headwind would mean a delay to enable it to fly across the Sinai desert and reach Egypt.

There was nothing in Gaza itself to tempt you there so our only off duty entertainment was the NAAFI on the main camp and an open-air cinema. This consisted of a mud brick walled area with a white cloth screen on a wooden frame. There was a small selection of films. My favourite was a Western, which had suffered many splits and patches. This meant that the inevitable horseback chase was frequently interrupted by short sequences of two men rowing a boat across an open sea! Even this entertainment came to an abrupt end in a real-life desert storm, which wrecked the screen.

The camp cinema (after a gale), RAF Gaza, 1942.

RAF Gaza provided my first and only acquaintance with the RAF Regiment, affectionately known as "Rock Apes". Their function was to provide airfield protection. To this end they had a machine gun position at the edge of the airfield and they lived in a tent alongside. One night, to their extreme embarrassment, the tent was stolen from over their heads as they slept. Fortunately for them, their arms and ammunition were not taken as well.

The battle of Alamein

On 23 October 1942 the Battle of Alamein commenced. Gradually the stack of fighter aircraft was run down until all were gone. Unbeknown to us, a large store of bombs and ammunition had been assembled in a desert location nearby. Lads from the Station were used as armed escorts on the convoys assembled and dispatched to the battle zone. These took around seven days to travel down into Egypt, across the Suez Canal and up into the Western Desert. When they returned, they told us that the planning and logistics were so good that they were arriving at their intended destinations within hours of the areas being cleared of enemy forces. This was achieved without the use of computers and with very basic communications.

Through November and December, the battle area moved ever westwards and, for us, everything went very quiet. With the help of the NAAFI staff, we began to save our meagre beer ration for Christmas. We also wondered what would become of us.

Christmas in Gaza, 1942

Eventually Christmas came and the RAF Station staff managed to make room for our small contingent to move into proper wooden huts with real beds and electric light for Christmas and Boxing Day. As for our carefully saved beer supplies, the 9th Australian Division had been withdrawn from the fighting and pulled back to our area. They got wind of our stock of beer, descended on us like a plague of locusts and drank the camp dry! We consoled ourselves with the fact that they deserved it, having taken the brunt of the fighting in one part of the Alamein battle and suffered heavy casualties.

CHRISTMAS DAY MENU RAF GAZA 1942

A parade to remember

Christmas over, we were back to our Spartan life in the Nissen hut. At the beginning of January 1943, we were told that the aforementioned Australian Army Division was to be reviewed by General Alexander, Commander in Chief Middle East Forces, prior to their return to Australia. The parade would be held on our airfield and, as hosts to the event, a Flight of 30 airmen would be included. For some reason I was selected as one of that number.

By that time, due to the necessary priority given to fighting equipment and materials in the build-up to Alamein, our stores were virtually empty. It being winter, our uniform was khaki battledress and consisted of the most amazing assortment of ill-fitting garments you ever did see. For instance, although only a Leading Aircraftsman, I had been given an olive green jacket of American origin.

The great day came and we made ourselves as presentable as possible in the circumstances. The parade itself followed a similar pattern to that of the Sovereign's Birthday parade with a review by General Alexander, followed by a march past in slow time, then in quick time and a final march off. We were included in the review and then became spectators until the march off.

For the review, the general stood in an open jeep and was driven slowly past each contingent. He was immaculate, as indeed were all the Australian soldiery. What on earth went through his mind when, at the very end of his tour he was confronted by our motley squad of oddly-attired airmen I cannot guess but to his credit not a flicker of amazement or amusement crossed his face. And I can assure you that in spite of our dishevelled appearance, as we brought up the rear of the parade when we marched off, our marching and salute would have been a credit to a Guards platoon, despite our having been on the parade ground for the best part of five hours.

The parade itself was the most moving experience of my life. The Aussies had not been sorted out into neat, full-sized platoons but were in their individual units. Some were more or less full-size but many were just a dozen or less men. The smallest I can remember was only three. As they went marching proudly by, colours flying and heads held high, I felt proud and privileged to be there to share that moment with them. Even now, when I watch the Queen's Birthday Parade on Horseguards, I think of them and of their many comrades who did not make it to that ceremony.

An angel of mercy

Not long afterwards I suffered an attack of jaundice and was sent to a tented Army Field Hospital at Rafah. Being the only airman among about 30 army lads, I was the butt of all the usual ribaldry. However, we all adored our lovely English Nursing Sister. Just imagine her impact on such young lads in their late teens or twenties, most of whom had not seen such a young woman for years. The most fearsome battleaxe would have seemed an angel in those circumstances!

My only complaint during my ten days stay was that, having jaundice, I was not allowed the daily ration of half a pint of Guinness.

Army Field Hospital at Rafah in the Sinai Desert, February 1942/3 (with our lovely Ward Sister!)

A good pair of boots

The only other matter of note was that my RAF boots finally gave up the struggle and fell apart. I was issued with a pair of army ammunition boots. This heavy and well-studded footwear belied its appearance and was as comfortable as could be. What is more, they lasted the remaining 2½ years until I arrived home without any repairs whatsoever. In fact,

I was sorry to have to give them up and return to the RAF version.

The author, wearing an elegant hospital 'blues' suit, possibly Boer War vintage! February 1943.

Netanya

From there I was sent to Netanya, a seaside resort, north of Tel Aviv, for a week of convalescence. The main memories I have are of its superb beach of firm sand and a delicious sweet white wine, which helped the evenings pass in a most delightful way. Fortunately there was no one to remind me that I should not be drinking alcohol!

In February 1993, Netanya was the last stop on a coach tour of Israel my wife and I were enjoying. I was so looking forward to revisiting the places I could remember – and maybe a glass or two of that white wine. We arrived at our hotel on the seafront just as a storm force gale right off the sea was building up. Consequently, it was impossible to go out of the door and we spent most of the evening sitting in candlelight due to a power cut!

My convalescence over, it was back to Gaza once again to be told that I was to report to Air Headquarters Levant in Jerusalem. A posting to a Balloon Squadron in Haifa had come in while I was in hospital and I was now on my way to replace an airman from HQ who had taken my place. The unit was being brought up to strength before moving to the Western Desert. For me, this turned out to be doubly fortunate. Firstly, it gave me a spell in what was by far the most interesting city in the whole of the Middle East. Secondly, I discovered very much later that the balloon squadron was in the first wave ashore in the Sicilian invasion to provide protection from attacks by low flying aircraft.

Fallen comrades

Before moving on from Gaza, I must mention our severe losses from a unit only about 30 strong. Three of our wireless operators, who were manning a direction-finding van based in the hills near Hebron, were murdered one night. The perpetrators of this attack were never found but throughout the war the Jewish Stern gang and other insurgents were active and a constant threat. The other casualty was a young lad who developed diabetes. I do not know if insulin was available in the UK in those days, but even if it had been there was no way of getting it to him in time to save him. He was a quiet lad, an only child of an elderly couple, and we all felt very much for them in their loss. I pay tribute to them all and their sacrifice.

Air Headquarters Levant, Jerusalem

Air headquarters personnel were billeted in a wing of the Convent of Notre Dame, opposite the New Gate of the Old City, Jerusalem. The Nuns had long departed. Visiting Israel in 1993, I found that the United Nations Peacekeeping force were based there and their guardroom was the same building that we had used, except that all the windows were now of bulletproof glass! No doubt they are still there.

I duly reported to the Guard Room on arrival, in my usual strange mix of ragged uniform clothing. The Unit Warrant Officer was there and stared at me in utter disbelief.

"Where the (expletive deleted) have you come from airman?" he said.

"Gaza Sir, where the stores have had no clothing for months," said I, standing smartly to attention all the while.

I was ordered to go straight to the Stores for all the new kit I needed, as I could not go around Air Headquarters looking like that. It was my first indication that I was now in a completely different world to that I had experienced so far in the Middle East.

Having made myself more presentable in my new uniform, I reported to the Orderly Room, as one does, fully expecting that to be my new workplace, but to my surprise I was told to report to the Intelligence Section in Air Headquarters at 8am the next morning.

Notre Dame Convent Jerusalem 1943.
Living quarters for Air HQ Levant staff.

The Author standing beside the United Nations Guard Room, 1993.

The intelligence section

Me? Intelligence? Was I destined to become an undercover spy? I probably wondered, or hoped, that I might even be working with some glamorous Mata Hari type female agent! My head full of this surmising, I took myself off to my new quarters, a comfortable room, standard bed with three 'biscuit'-type mattresses, blankets and crisp white sheets! Even a bedside table and somewhere to store my kit. After the previous 18 months it was so unexpected I even forgot about Mata Hari.

Next morning I was up at 06.30 hours, breakfasted (proper tables and chairs!) and away down the quarter of a mile or so to Air Headquarters, opposite the Damascus Gate of the Old City. [In 1993 this had returned to its' normal use as a Boys School.]

Former Air Headquarters Building in 1993, now in use as a Boys' School.

On booking-in at the Guard Room, I was directed to the first floor. Finding the appropriately marked door, I knocked and entered this supposed hub of spying and undercover activity. It was a fairly large room with an inner sanctum, this being the domain of a Flight Lieutenant Intelligence Officer. The remainder of the department was just me – Leading Aircraftsman, tea boy, receptionist, minder of persons wanting to see my boss, and general factotum (i.e. 'dogsbody'). Definitely no Mata Haris!

Information gathering

One very important on-going activity was the encouragement of any Jewish residents with links to Germany to give us any holiday postcards, snapshots or other useful information they might have. From the mass of material that came in, we sorted out anything that might be a potential air raid target and sent it by the fastest available method to the United Kingdom. This included many different postcard views of the dams which were later the targets of the famous "Dambuster" raids. We were also given detailed plans of the very important ball-bearing factory in Schweinfurt, indicating the key target areas to achieve maximum effect. The ball bearings produced by this factory were a vital component for the German aircraft industry as well as other armaments. An air raid was carried out on 14th October 1943, which caused considerable destruction and disruption of output and led to the Germans widely dispersing future production facilities.

Another daily task was to read the local newspaper "Palestine Post" (which was printed in English) and take cuttings of any references to the RAF or which may be of particular interest to the Air Officer Commanding.

A well-intentioned deception

I also had to maintain the large noticeboard in the entrance hall, which contained a selection of press photographs with appropriate captions. These were always received months after the event. As a view of bomb damage of one Arab town looked much like any other, I decided, for morale boosting purposes of course, to change the captions to places we had captured just 7-10 days before.

One morning I was putting up a fresh set when the Air Officer Commanding came in. I sprang smartly to attention while he examined my work. He looked me straight in the eye and said, "These photographs are coming through much more quickly now, aren't they?"

"Yes sir," said I – but I think I had been rumbled!

Learning to speak German

After a few months, my boss decided that it would be a good idea if I learnt German. I think this was to enable me to interrogate German Prisoners, though where these would come from was hard to imagine, as the conflict had now moved to Sicily and Italy. However, off I went to the Berlitz school of Languages in Jerusalem one evening a week. It was a strange experience as I was the odd one out in a class of Jewish civilians, who were not really into fraternising with English servicemen.

A historic opportunity

Due to our split working hours of mornings and evenings, I had two hours or more free each afternoon and on Sundays, our half day, from 1pm. I was literally just across the road from the Old City, a fascinatingly interesting tourist destination that, in peacetime, drew people in from all over the world. This enabled me to explore every accessible inch and to get to know the whole area really well. There being no tourists about, I could spend time walking the Via Dolorosa, or the different market areas, or visiting the Holy Sepulchre, the Western (Wailing) Wall and many other sites, just soaking up the atmosphere.

On Sunday afternoons, an Armenian gentlemen who worked for the Palestine Post offered free guided tours. About a dozen servicemen like myself were his regular customers. The many others stationed in Jerusalem did not realize what they were missing. He varied the itinerary to cover the Old City and destinations in surrounding areas that could be reached by foot or on public transport.

Under his guidance we visited well known sites such as Bethlehem and the Church of the Nativity, Ein Karem, the Mount of Olives and the Garden of Gethsemane. Others were less well known, such as Hezekiah's Tunnel. This was built about 700BC to bring water from the Gihon Spring in the Kidron Valley to the east of the Old City, passing under the city to the Pool of Siloam to the west. The water is about knee deep. A group of Arab women doing their laundry in the pool were taken by surprise by our sudden appearance out of the Tunnels.

Another day we walked the valley from north to south, past all the old burial caves in the valley walls. At the end an old, roofless, Crusader Church was completely filled with the bones of the long deceased that had been removed from the caves to make room for the new arrivals.

An interrupted train journey

One extremely memorable trip was to Latrun Monastery, founded by French Trappist Monks and about 30 km from Jerusalem on the railway line to Tel Aviv. We had a very pleasant afternoon there, enjoying the gardens and surrounding views. We caught the return train about 6pm, consisting of two coaches hauled by a steam locomotive. Progress was slow, as it was uphill all the way and the train was packed with families, probably returning from a day at the coast.

Suddenly, the train came to a juddering halt. Flames were seen coming from the oil-fired locomotive. Practically all the adults jumped down on the track, leaving their scared children behind! We lifted them all down, checking through the coaches as we did so, and then went to check on the driver. He had managed to slam on the brakes and shut off the fractured oil feed pipe, suffering badly burnt hands in the process. The guard told us that a relief engine would come down from Jerusalem to take the train on, but it would take several hours.

As there was nothing more that we could do there and it was almost dark, we decided to walk back, no easy task on a pitch-black night. We eventually made it back a little after 10pm, by which time the Services Clubs and Canteens had all shut! As we made our way back, we saw no sign of another engine going to the rescue.

The Dead Sea

The other outing of note was one to the Dead Sea, organised among ourselves. We did all the normal touristy thing of having a float on the water, a weird experience indeed. The density of the water makes it impossible to swim. Nowadays the Dead Sea is shrinking fast. The main source of replenishment is the River Jordan, which runs down from the Sea of Galilee (Lake Tiberius), a freshwater lake fed by the runoff from the Golan Heights and Syrian Mountains to the north. Water extraction by both Israel and Jordan has diminished the flow into the Dead Sea considerably.

Air HQ Levant staff outing to the Dead Sea, 1943.

Floating in the Dead Sea, 1943.

All good things...

I enjoyed this pleasant life as much as I could, knowing it would not last forever. Towards the end of September, I was put on standby to go to Kos, one of the Dodecanese Islands off the Turkish coast, which we had just retaken. Hopefully it was not the intention that I should interrogate any Germans taken prisoner, as my linguistic skills acquired to date would hardly have enabled me to ask them whether they would like tea or coffee or to offer them a cigarette! The island was the only one in the group with an airfield and so of great strategic importance. As a result, the Germans counter-attacked with such speed it was recaptured before I had even been told to pack my bags.

Posted to Syria

Eventually the call came in early November. Seven of us were detailed to be an advance party for the formation of an Advanced Air Headquarters in northern Syria. We were to fly from Lydda to Aleppo and prepare for the remaining personnel to arrive in about seven days' time. I know we were in the RAF, but in those days transport by air for personnel like us was unheard of, so it must have been urgent. Early the next morning we were to travel to Lydda by the normal "back of a 3-ton truck" mode. There we were told we would be put on a Blenheim bomber.

An uncomfortable plane ride

There was a Sergeant, a Corporal and five other ranks, and I was by far the junior of those five. The Blenheim, being only a light aircraft, had very little space to accommodate seven passengers and their kit, in addition to the crew. As a result I was allocated the most remote, cramped and uncomfortable space you could imagine. For all I knew, it might have been in the bomb bay and I spent the whole flight with my fingers crossed, hoping that no one would press the wrong button and open the bomb bay doors, especially as none of us had parachutes!

After a long, very cold and bumpy ride, we landed at Aleppo and I managed to climb out of my hell-hole and feel the most welcome *terra firma* under my feet. We were put in the normal, furniture-less shed for the night and were told we would be taken to our allocated area the next day. I was back to Spartan life again – with a vengeance.

Advanced Air Headquarters, Aleppo

The next day we were taken to a barren and rather rocky area just north of the city, alongside the railway line to Turkey. It contained a few tents and was to be our home for months to come. Most days a freight train rattled by, with tanks, armoured cars and other military equipment boldly marked with banners proclaiming "Aid to Turkey". RAF personnel were sometimes used as armed escorts, one per flatbed wagon and totally exposed to the elements. We heard that one of them had fallen asleep, or more likely frozen up in the bitter weather, and had been carried over the border into Turkey. This should have meant internment, but the Turkish authorities were not known for their strict application of such matters, so he returned a few days later.

Spartan conditions

In the ten days or so it took for our main party to be assembled and arrive by road, a squad of Free French Senegalese troops arrived and built a couple of corrugated iron huts for us. No fancy work here: a concrete base and wood frame clad in sheets of corrugated iron. Windowless, the only ventilation was via a wooden-framed section which could be pushed outwards but never was. There were so many gaps where the iron sheets met, it was hardly necessary anyway.

Heating was to be by a diesel-fuelled, drip-feed stove, which was so ineffective and potentially dangerous that it was hardly ever used; lighting was provided by a few hurricane lamps. Our two cooks performed miracles in a canvas-sided cooking trailer designed for use in the desert. Water was rationed and came from a water bowser but the only means of heating it was by a diesel drip-feed boiler, which ensured that the tea was always diesel-flavoured. The ablutions and latrines were inevitably open-air. Cut down empty fuel cans were used as washbasins and hot (or even warm) water was non- existent. The command hub for this empire was in a desert-style communications trailer, containing the Commanding Officer, Adjutant, Unit Warrant Officer, Radio Officers and me.

We were totally unprepared for the weather about to hit us in December. From about the middle of the month, the temperature dropped well below zero, day and night, for six weeks or more. The prevailing wind from the north just added to the chill factor. Virtually everyone, cooks included, worked, ate and slept fully-clothed, with greatcoats, balaclava helmets and mittens. These latter items had been knitted by good ladies at home as comforts for the troops. They certainly did the job for us, but how they came to be in the Middle East, not normally regarded as a cold-weather area, is a mystery.

As 'cold weather rations', our normal two slices of bread a day was increased to three, plus a mug of cocoa (diesel-flavoured, of course) and without milk. The concrete floor of the hut was always damp, so we improvised beds with sheets of corrugated iron balanced on empty petrol cans. The cooks did their best to give us a hot meal, but the food congealed on our tin plates in the short distance from the cooking trailer to the hut, where we did have some folding wooden tables and forms. The bread was always infested with weevils (fortunately cooked, not alive). At first some tried picking them out, but there were so many and bread was rationed, so we just consoled ourselves with the fact that they were extra protein and ate them. The margarine, runny in warm weather, was a solid block and had to be chiselled out and put on the bread in chunks.

Despite all the difficulties and discomforts, we all got on with our jobs to the best of our abilities. You should have seen me, with frozen fingers, trying to type Daily Routine Orders, that essential item of service life. There was no moaning or groaning, there was a war on, so we just got on with it.

At least mail from home was getting through fairly regularly and within about two weeks of being posted, which was a big boost to our morale. Before the Mediterranean had been opened up, the mail had travelled by ship around the Cape and had taken six weeks or more to arrive, except for the little one-page 'aerogrammes', which were photographed and sent by plane as a reel of film, to be developed and printed at their destination, which took about three weeks.

Life was pretty dire but the bright spot every week was our half-day off on Sunday. We were about three miles from

Aleppo, so it was within walking distance. Early on, we found a very ordinary French-style café/bar which became a regular haunt. For a few hours we enjoyed warmth, light, a friendly welcome and mouth-watering baguette-style sandwiches, not to mention a very smooth local red wine.

Christmas in Syria, 1943

With Christmas approaching, we asked the proprietor if he could do a Christmas meal for us. He agreed and quoted an all-inclusive price of 5 shillings a head. A majority of the unit personnel, about two dozen in total, signed up for the deal and it was arranged for the Sunday before Christmas.

The great day arrived and we set off in great anticipation. When we opened the door and trooped in, we were astounded. The place had been transformed. The individual tables had been pushed together in two rows and were dressed with immaculate snow-white table linen, serviettes and polished silver cutlery and glassware, all borrowed from a nearby hotel. Christmas decorations were all around, with the boss and all the staff lined up to greet us. The meal itself was magnificent, the full traditional fare with wine and beer and coffee to follow. How they managed it in the depths of the war and all its restrictions, I do not know.

On Christmas Day we had our own Christmas Dinner, served by our two officers, as is the tradition. It could not match the earlier one but our cooks achieved miracles from their desert trailer galley, against all the odds.

Advanced Air Headquarters Staff, Christmas 1943, North of Aleppo, Syria.

Spitfire Day, Aleppo 1944 – to raise funds to build new planes.

How I Got My Knees Brown ~ 55

My permanent pass for the year 1944 at Advanced Air Headquarters.

My 21st birthday, Aleppo 1944

The next milestone in my life was my 21st birthday, on 16th February 1944. Things were beginning to wind down a bit by then, so I must have been able to wangle a half-day off for myself and some of my pals, to enable us to repair to our favourite bar in town and duly celebrate.

My enduring memories of the evening were of climbing on the policeman's rostrum in the centre of a crossroads and directing the non-existent traffic, followed by creeping up to the side door of a hall which was strictly 'out of bounds' to us, opening it and finding that it opened onto the side of a stage where a well-proportioned lady was doing a belly dance. We shut the door and scarpered speedily. I had the impression that the lady had given us a wave, but that was probably my imagination.

After all these excitements, and to celebrate the importance of the occasion, we decided to take a horse-drawn 'gharry' back to camp. Full of my own importance, I climbed up alongside the driver to give directions. After flinging my left arm out just as we turned right and being saved from a dive into the ditch by a quick grab from the cabbie, I decided to leave it to him and/or his horse, who probably knew the road rather better than I did.

Operation Saturn

Needless to say that, it being wartime, we did not really know why we were there. We assumed it was to do with a possible German attack through Turkey. Three Fighter squadrons had flown into the airfield from Italy and when we saw any of the lads in Aleppo, they would use their bragging rights about life in the front line while we had been swanning around in the comfort and safety of the Middle East!

Only long after the war, when reading Winston Churchill's book "The Second World War" did I discover what had really been going on. Apparently, there had been several other attempts to persuade Turkey to enter the war on our side. Several airfields had been built there and military equipment such as tanks and anti-aircraft guns had been supplied. British service personnel had been working in the country in civilian clothes as technicians and training Turkish troops.

We had seen some of our lads in civvies going in that direction and many more coming back when Operation 'Saturn', as it was known, was called off. I was a bit sceptical of this 'disguise', as all personnel were dressed in grey flannel trousers and sports jackets – brown for the army and air force blue for the RAF! The proposed date for the operation to begin was 15th February, the eve of my 21st birthday. Had it gone ahead, I would certainly have had a 21st to remember!

An amazing coincidence

One other occurrence of note during my Aleppo experience was when I was sent to the nearest field hospital as I was running a very high temperature. There was a short queue at the reception desk. The orderly taking my details did not look up until I gave him my name.

Then came instant recognition. It was George Palk, a fellow chorister at St Peter's church in Shaldon.

Much later, I learnt that news of this incident had reached the pages of our local newspaper. Being wartime, it did not say where it had happened, just "somewhere in the Middle East".

> **Shaldon Reunion In M.E.**
>
> An unexpected meeting between two young men from Shaldon recently took place in the Middle East. L.A.C. Rupert Extence, R.A.F., son of Mr. R. Extence, of Daymor House, Shaldon, in hospital, suddenly saw Pte. G. C. Palk, R.A.M.C., writing at a desk. Pte. Palk, son of Councillor and Mrs. E. J Palk, was organist at St. Peter's Church, Shaldon, and L.A.C. Extence sang in the choir.

Cutting from the Shaldon local paper.

A night out in Beirut

As we moved towards the end of February, the weather started warming up and life became quite pleasant again. However, there no longer being any need for an Advanced Air Headquarters, it was 'pack up and go' time. Our small convoy moved off to the south, for a night stop in Beirut. Knowing the city well, I suggested a visit to a café/bar that I knew well. About a dozen of us went off to seek a quiet drink and a bite to eat. On entering, shock-horror, it was now a brothel! I had not realised that "Monty" [Field Marshal Sir Bernard Montgomery] on taking command of the Middle East forces, had closed down all such establishments. Previously in Beirut they had been legal, licensed, regulated, regularly inspected and concentrated in one area. Inevitably, I suppose, they had gone undercover throughout the city. We gave up the idea of finding somewhere for a quiet drink.

The next morning we were on the road again, travelling south over the beautiful coastal road to Palestine, that was to become the site of more fighting and bombardment in later years between Israeli and Lebanese forces. Once back in Palestine we were dispersed to our various new units, saving me from many months of ribbing about my choice of venue for an evening out!

120 Maintenance Unit, Ras el Ain, Palestine

My destination was 120 Maintenance Unit at Ras el Ain, a huge dispersed store depot with a 12-mile perimeter fence situated about five miles east of Petah Tiqva, a town reputed to be the location of the headquarters of the Stern Gang, the largest and most active Jewish terrorist organisation (self-styled 'freedom fighters').

After Aleppo our Nissen Hut accommodation seemed luxurious; still no furniture but proper beds and heating, when the weather was cold enough to need it. I also discovered that Walter Stoneman, another Shaldon friend, was stationed there and we were able to move into the same hut. Almost as important, we were able to arrange that our nights on guard duty coincided, otherwise we would have very little off duty time to share.

Walter Stoneman, 120 Maintenance Unit. Ras el Ain, Palestine, 1944.

The toilets were of the 'deep hole' variety, which you could prove by dropping in a stone and noting the time it took to reach the bottom! You also had to look out for the snakes, which frequently came slithering around. Happily, they ignored you if you ignored them. Even so, it could be a bit disconcerting to encounter one as you sat there, attending to a call of nature and contemplating your future, past, or more likely what the next meal was likely to be.

Guarding the perimeter

Working hours were 8am to 5pm, with no break during the heat of the day, rather than the normal 8am to 1pm and 5pm to 8pm. Presumably this was to allow us the pleasure of guarding the perimeter every third night from 6pm to 6am! There was a double fence with a minefield in between, about 100 yards from the perimeter road and across very rough ground. There were 12 guard posts, about a mile apart, along the road, each being no more than a small tent with three camp beds. Each man patrolled for half a mile in each direction from his post for two hours twice during the night and spent the time in between trying to sleep, lying on his rifle [for security purposes]. The Corporal cat-napped in between supervising changeovers and dealing with any problems that might arise.

The whole operation required a roster from 36 corporals and 108 airmen, which was just about the full complement available. Sleeping on your rifle, uncomfortable as it might be, was preferable to a Court Martial if you had it stolen! That and your ammunition were reputed to be the main target for any thief managing to get past the perimeter fences. Certainly they would be the most readily portable and saleable items available. We were frequently reminded of this, possibly to encourage us to keep awake and alert while on patrol where we would probably be either killed or seriously injured in the attempted theft.

My guard post was in the middle of the northern side of the camp where a camel trail ran close to the fence. A road ran alongside the southern fence and the camp entrance. We kept the same post and personnel so that we knew the terrain and worked together as a team.

A shot in the dark

It was here that I fired my only shot in the whole war that was not in practice on a firing range. We were very used to hearing the soft padding of camels along the trail and the creaking of their harness. One dark, moonless night I could hear the sound of someone or something much closer moving towards me. I shouted the challenge "Halt! Who goes there, friend or foe?" There was no answer, but the noise stopped. I listened intently. After a minute or two I heard the sound again coming my way. Following the rules, I shouted "Halt, or I fire!" Silence once again, and then the noise once more. I took aim in the direction of the sounds and fired one round. Silence and no further noise.

Our Corporal came belting up and I explained what had happened. Shortly afterwards the Duty Officer came up in his pickup truck and we used the headlights to illuminate the area as best we could but could see nothing. They probably thought that I had panicked! Later on, just before dawn, my mate, who was on the 4am to 6am shift, heard movement, but as it was going away from him, he did not challenge but reported it to our Corporal. As soon as it was sufficiently light, we searched the area and found evidence of someone, probably an Arab, having hidden at the bottom of a gully. My reputation was restored!

Reflecting on the incident afterwards, I knew what to do if my first challenge had been answered "Friend". The correct reply was "Advance friend and be recognised". Nevertheless, it would have been difficult to keep him covered and carry out the identification check; I would have had to hope that my challenges had been sufficiently loud to bring reinforcements. I checked Kings Regulations to see what should be done if the answer to my first challenge had been "Foe" but found nothing. Presumably, it was assumed that nobody would ever be that daft!

To this day I get very angry when the usual armchair critics start pontificating about the actions taken by the Police when they have unfortunately killed or injured someone in similar circumstances. You feel very vulnerable indeed when you have to disclose your position when making the challenges. The critics should try it themselves sometime.

The sound of gunfire

On another night we also had a bit of excitement. All was quiet and still and the routine of patrolling was proceeding as usual when suddenly all hell broke loose on the opposite side of the camp and what is now known as a 'fire-fight' ensued for five minutes or so. The weaponry used in those days was much noisier than the modern equivalent, so it was quite impressive. We woke the two lads on their sleeping turn and stood to, in case the action came our way. Later on we were told that the Stern Gang had attacked the Palestine radio transmitter north of Jerusalem and the Palestine Police had set up a roadblock on the road running alongside the perimeter fence. Despite the impressive sound effects, as far as I know, no one was caught, killed or injured in this affray.

Beer and a singsong

For our two free evenings between guard duties, we did at least have a NAAFI canteen and a daily beer ration. The beer came in returnable bottles with a small refundable deposit. As we were paid fortnightly, to guard against having insufficient funds just before payday, my friend Walter and I had a system of storing the empties in a kitbag and taking them back at an appropriate time.

Our evening entertainment was invariably to have a singsong. Our large male voice choir was the best and most versatile I encountered in the whole of my RAF career. Our repertoire covered everything from the Edwardian Music Hall, First World War, between the wars and early Second World War. I say 'early' Second World War as most of us had been out of touch with the latest pop songs since 1941. A great favourite was one whose polite title was "Bless 'em All". One particular line of the chorus – "You'll get no promotion this side of the ocean" – was always sung with great gusto and meaningfulness.[1]

A promotion of sorts

Until the latter part of 1944, the normal policy was to fill NCO vacancies from personnel coming out from the UK. Perhaps we sang loudly enough to be heard. About two months after my joining the Unit, the Orderly Room Sergeant returned to the UK. I think he was a married man and only had a three-year deployment. We had no other NCO, so, as I was a "regular", an ex-apprentice and had long since risen to the dizzy heights of Leading Aircraftsman by dint of passing the necessary Trade Tests, I was given the job until the replacement came from the UK. Unfortunately, no extra pay, no acting rank and, above all, no relief from the regular round of guard duties. The only thing I did get was six weeks experience of running an Orderly Room with about eight staff.

The WAAF arrive

By early July our first contingent of WAAF personnel had arrived. Understandably, they were billeted about five miles away in the Petah Tiqva direction, hopefully not next door to

---

[1] Editor's note: 'Bless 'em All' is one of the many songs of the wartime RAF contained in *Bawdy Ballads & Dirty Ditties* (published by Woodfield) – a splendid and uncensored collection of the ribald rewordings of well-known songs that were a popular form of homemade entertainment for all ranks, as performed in RAF messes the world over during the wartime years.

the Stern Gang. From there they were ferried to and fro each day by the normal three-ton truck method. The bonus for us was that we could get a lift between the main gate and various dispersed work sites with them. Three very pleasant and efficient older (40ish) ladies were allocated to the Orderly Room. They were amazed that that a mere youngster like myself was a seasoned veteran of almost three years' service in the Middle east and five years overall. I received a certain amount of mothering from them. Another new experience!

I realised that once the WAAFs arrived it would not be long before I was on the move again. However, I stayed long enough to experience the first Camp Dance that was organised. Luckily, I was not on guard duty that night. Most of us had had no opportunity to socialize since leaving the UK, so it was a bit overpowering, but the girls did a brilliant job of putting us at our ease.

I had stayed sober and behaved impeccably, as far as I could remember, so do not think that my departure within a four or five days was related to that evening!

Moving on again

Four of five of us were dispatched on a three-tonner heading for Egypt. The distance meant a night stop half way across the Sinai Desert and a night sleeping under the stars. As ever when you stopped anywhere, no matter how remote, some Arabs appeared, looking for a chance to barter or some baksheesh. A tried and tested response to such entreaties was *"Anna maskeen, mafeesh filoose"* (I am poor and I have no money). Normally this was a pretty accurate statement anyway!

The next day it was back to that gem of the Middle East, Kasfareet Transit Camp. We were told that we were on our way to Italy. After almost three years of service at the eastern end of the Mediterranean, that could only be good news. We all began to dream of Italian towns and cities, as well as being a lot nearer to home.

As airmen who had "got their knees brown" (i.e. were seasoned veterans) we were excused the normal chores of tidying up the desert and given a 'plum job' – vegetable preparation for the Sergeants' Mess! There followed blissful days of sitting in the shade outside the cookhouse peeling spuds in the middle of an Egyptian heatwave, with temperatures around 122-124°F (50°C). However, there was one important perk; having shown such expertise in helping to prepare the meals, we were allowed to eat there rather than partake of whatever was being provided for the lower orders.

Then, for me, came bad news. I was no longer going to Italy. For some unknown reason my presence was required in Aden. Not only had I been I totally unimpressed by the place when we called there on the way out, it was very much further from home than Italy. However, as a popular saying of the time put it – "Ours is not to reason why; ours is but to do or die" or alternatively "If you can't take a joke, you shouldn't have joined!"

Within a few days I was back on the road south to Port Tewfik and boarding a Far East bound troopship, this time the *Strathaird*. There followed three days of cruising southward, to constant reminders not to be in the sun and that severe sunburn would be treated as a self-inflicted injury. After years in the desert I was well aware of that fact and had no need to top up my existing suntan, which by then was mahogany brown!

Air Headquarters, Aden

Arriving at anchorage off Aden Port, I was ferried ashore and taken to Air Headquarters. This was situated at Steamer Point, a large headland to seaward of the port, and was part way up the hill, just below the RAF hospital, the main hospital for the Aden Command area.

On reporting to the Orderly Room I was told that I was to be posted to an RAF Staging Post on Masirah Island, just off the coast of Oman, about 1000 miles to the northeast. The only link to it was an elderly Wellington bomber, which spent its declining years transporting mail and supplies to various far-flung destinations. It paid a weekly visit to Masirah, but its limited capacity meant that I had been booked on a flight in November, about ten weeks ahead. Meanwhile, I would be treated as supernumerary, that is to say, given any old job that cropped up.

Headquarters Aden Command staff, 1945.

Too darn hot

To set the scene, Aden was scenically, climatically and in every other way, the pits! So much so that time spent there was counted as double towards the completion of your tour and in any event should not exceed one year. That was the theory, but unfortunately in wartime, not always the practice. In my year there, the temperature day and night stayed within a few degrees either side of 95°F (35°C) and the humidity level was constantly very high. The sun rose each day around 6am and set around 6pm, and in-between there was scarcely ever a cloud in the sky. Air conditioning was unheard of, and the slow-moving ceiling fans we had simply stirred the hot, humid air. The only rain I saw was a few large spots on Christmas morning 1944, but these evaporated the moment they hit the hot, dusty ground. Gastric problems were commonplace, as was 'prickly heat', a very itchy rash caused by the humidity. Nowadays I expect life there is much more comfortable, with air conditioning and all the mod cons.

Brown knees & pith helmets, Aden 1944.

The accommodation

The Headquarters, Hospital and barrack blocks were reputed to have been built by prisoners of war, presumably from Napoleonic times, which would put them in the same category as Dartmoor Prison. The rooms were quite spacious, with fairly high ceilings, a blessing in that climate. The beds were Indian style wooden *charpoys*, comfortable enough but a haven for bedbugs. A weekly debugging session was essential but only provided a brief respite from their attentions.

The food

The cookhouse was on the opposite side of an open quadrangle from the Airmen's Mess, presumably to distance it from the heat of the kitchen area. I cannot imagine what it must have been like to work there. The meal of the day was frequently a goat meat stew with onions, rice and sweet potato. We did have a roast on Sundays, and butter, often rancid, instead of margarine for our weevil-infested bread. Obviously, we had to collect our food from one side of the quadrangle to take it to the other to eat. This was enlivened by the presence of a flock of large, seagull-type birds, who did their best to grab what they could on the way. It would be impolite to tell you the name we gave them.

Recreation

About the only recreation we had was swimming, which we did most afternoons from a small beach at the foot of Steamer Point. It was protected by shark netting, so we swam happily and with confidence until one day when the tide went right out and we saw holes in the fence you could drive a double decker bus through. It did not stop us swimming, but we did so with great circumspection after that.

Aden was a long established peacetime base and had a Sailing Club. I had had the opportunity of going for a sail one afternoon, a delightful and peaceful experience. My main memory is of a huge stingray basking in the sun on the surface. It needed no "Do not disturb" notice to keep us at a safe distance.

Swimming at steamer point, Aden, 1944.

Something to send home

There was little to tempt us down to the town, except one store which sold silk stockings at ridiculously cheap prices, there having been no civilian liners calling at the port on passage to and from India and the Far East for five years at least. These were very light and fitted easily into an envelope to send home, to the great delight of wives and girlfriends who deserved a treat for keeping us supplied with morale boosting and eagerly awaited letters from home.

Still work to be done...

But there was still a war on and our part in it was chiefly involved in dealing with the threat posed by Japanese submarines operating in the area, maintaining local and long distance supply routes by air and sea, and keeping a discrete eye on any troublemakers in our very large geographical area. In short, there was plenty of work to do.

The first job I was given was in the underground bunker which served as an operations and communication centre. It was in a small room lit by a single 40-watt bulb and furnished with one typewriter, a table and chair.

In this Spartan cell, my task was to receive messages decoded by the cipher officers next door, type them up and prepare them for distribution to the appropriate recipients.

Due to the onerous climatic conditions in Aden, this was organised on a 24-hour coverage of 6 hourly shifts with a 30-hour break after the night shift. However, it was not long before sickness and staff shortages brought it to 8-hour shifts with just one 24-hour break. That was really hard going.

Promotion and a lucky escape

Around the middle of October, that much-criticised overseas promotion policy mentioned earlier was changed and I became a corporal almost overnight. This not only increased my pay but also relieved me of my underground purgatory and, as it turned out, saved my life because it meant I would now not be among those sent to relieve the long-suffering airmen in Masirah. This was lucky for me because the flight in November on which I had been booked to travel crashed in a desolate mountainous area en route, killing all on board.

Now I was corporal, but still a supernumerary one, and likely to remain so for the rest of my time in Aden. It is a strange feeling having no specific job to do, perhaps a bit like being a "temp" nowadays. However, with my time in Aden counting as double, I would be due to return to the UK in February, something which would have been right out of the question had I gone to Masirah.

Funeral duty

Being located next door to the RAF hospital, it fell to Air Headquarters to provide a funeral party whenever required. Due to the climate, funerals always took place without delay and were normally held at either 6am or 6pm, to avoid the heat of the day. This meant that a permanent funeral party, comprising a Corporal, six airmen and a driver was required, the personnel involved being changed every six weeks.

The War Graves Cemetery was situated at the bottom of the aptly-named Silent Valley, a steep, rocky-sided cleft in the Aden peninsular; dry, barren and desolate, without a scrap of greenery. It must be one of the most difficult of such cemeteries in the world for relatives and friends to visit. I have seen fairly recent photos of it and, despite its location, it is immaculately maintained.

The funeral routine was a 5am call, meet the lads at the Armoury, draw rifles and blank ammunition and parade for inspection and checking of arms. Our hearse was a 15cwt pickup truck, which we would take to the Hospital Mortuary, where the Padre would be waiting with the coffin.

We would take up the coffin and process in slow time to the truck, load it and climb aboard, the Padre sitting in the cab with the driver. On arrival at the Cemetery, we would process to the graveside, led by the Padre. The driver would follow with our caps and rifles.

The funeral service would begin and, at the committal, we would take up the ropes and lower the coffin into the grave. Then we would take up our rifles and follow the necessary drill movements to the firing position and fire the salute. "Load, fire, reload, fire," until completed. The Lee Enfield rifles were much noisier than modern arms and each salvo fired would echo eerily around the valley sides.

Then it was "Caps on" and we would march back to the truck. The drive back to the Armoury was always quiet and I, for one, would be thinking of the deceased, even though it was someone I had never known. Then, after cleaning, checking and returning the arms, it was off to breakfast and a day's work. Even though there was not a solitary soul watching the proceedings, they were always carried out smartly, to the best of our ability, in accordance with British Military tradition.

Our first two funerals, on consecutive mornings, were those of two 18-year-old lads who had been brought ashore from a troopship en route to India, suffering from severe sunstroke, presumably having ignored the frequent warnings about excessive sunbathing on deck, especially when coming down the Red Sea. How sad that was.

Sixty-five years later, the repatriation ceremonies at RAF Lyneham and subsequent funerals of servicemen and women who had given their lives in Afghanistan brought it all back to me and I found myself waking at night and running through in my mind all the routine and drill involved.

Christmas in Aden, 1944

I would like to say that Christmas Day dawned bright and clear, but it didn't. It was hot and humid like any other. At least it was not several degrees below freezing, as it had been the year before in Aleppo. Traditionally the day saw a Carnival procession around Steamer Point. It was neither large nor colourful but a change from the normal routine. The most notable event was the few spots of rain I mentioned earlier.

As ever, we enjoyed a full Christmas dinner, which we guarded ever more closely from the marauding gulls!

The arrival of the New Year was greeted by the sound of sirens and fog horns from all the shipping in the port or anchored offshore. Other than that, it was just an ordinary working day.

My birthday in February came and went without the slightest sign that I would be doing anything other than staying where I was for a long time to come.

VE Day

On the 8th May, VE Day brought the war in Europe to an end but because we were on the fringe of the Far East conflict, with the possibility of Japanese submarines still operating in the shipping lanes, our war just carried on. In more recent times these same waters have been the haunt of the Somalian pirates.

I stand in for the warrant officer

Our Air Headquarters Warrant Officer was in hospital for several weeks and it fell to me to carry out some of his duties. As we were few in number and a pretty well-behaved lot on the whole, only once was I required to parade a defaulter in front of our Commanding Officer for judgement. I was well versed in the routine, having served as an escort to the accused on an almost daily basis earlier in my career at aircrew Initial Training Wing in Newquay.

The charge was quite serious, that of refusing to obey an order, and the fact that we were technically on active service made it even worse. However, acceptance of guilt and a show of remorse would probably have enabled our CO to pass a sentence of 14 days confinement to camp or "jankers" in common parlance.

I marched the accused and his escort in and halted them in front of the CO. The CO read out the charge and asked the accused if he had anything to say. He had plenty and was unrepentant, belligerent and downright 'bolshie'. In other words, he asked for what he got, which was 28 days detention, that is to say incarceration in a Military Prison. I marched him out in a state of shock, not for him, but for the problem that confronted me.

It was already about 10.30 and the Detention Centre was about half a mile away on the level ground at the bottom of the hill. They only accepted new prisoners between 6am and 12 noon daily. If I was unable to get him there by then, I faced the problem of keeping him under close arrest overnight, and we didn't even have the luxury of a cell to keep him in. I found a second escort and sent him off with the two of them to pack his kit, including backpack, and present himself in full marching order. Meanwhile, there was all the necessary paperwork to be prepared and signed by the CO, and no one else but me could do it.

Eventually we got it all together and set off, escorts, prisoner and myself, at the double down the hill in the heat and humidity of the day. For the prisoner it was a foretaste of things to come, for he would be doing everything at the double for the next 28 days. We reached our destination with five minutes to spare, marched him into Reception and halted him in front of the Reception Clerk's desk. The necessary process had begun when the prisoner suddenly grabbed an inkwell (no biros in those days) and emptied its contents over the clerk's head! That must have guaranteed him an even tougher 28 days. What a relief it was to get out of there. All three of us were shattered but still managed to march back up the hill in an orderly fashion.

The end of hostilities

The days and weeks dragged by ever more slowly until, suddenly, the war was over. A gruesome war ended in a gruesome manner by the second atom bomb in three days. Terrible though it was, at least it saved the lives of tens of thousands on both sides of the conflict had it dragged on longer. Above all, it released from purgatory thousands upon thousands of prisoners of war, many of whom might not have survived the conditions they were in for much longer.

Surely, I would be on my way home soon now? But no, the Air Officer Commanding Aden Command decreed that no one would be replaced until their WAAF replacements arrived. At the earliest, this would not be until November. What could I do?

I thought hard and long and decided that the only thing to do was to write home to my mother and ask her to put my case to her MP. Presumably letters would no longer be censored, but to be on the safe side I used one of the special green envelopes that were only subject to a random check. Normally these were only used to communicate with wives or girlfriends and were probably more interesting than all the other letters put together! I waited with trepidation for the result.

Waiting to go home

Shipping convoys no longer being needed, troopships no longer called at Aden on their way to India and the Far East and any homeward-bound vessels would be at full capacity with returning troops and released prisoners of war. Our only link with Egypt was an elderly and small troopship, the SS *Dilwara*, which made regular round trips from Port Tewfik to Mombasa and back, calling at various ports en route. She called at Aden once every six weeks and was next due at the beginning of September. The days came and went and I was beginning to resign myself to a long wait before I would begin my journey home.

Suddenly on the 1st of September we received a long message direct from the Air Ministry. That, in itself, was quite an event. Normally everything was channelled through Air Headquarters Middle East in Cairo. It gave explicit instructions that all time-expired personnel were to be repatriated at the first possible opportunity. It then provided a list of all those concerned in order, by date, of their embarkation from the UK. And there, at the top by some distance, was my number, rank, name and the date 15.8.1941. I could not believe my eyes, went hot and cold and experienced a host of different emotions. The *Dilwara* was due to sail in a couple of days. Could I possibly be on it?

3. The Long Journey Home

As soon as a copy hit the Air Officer Commanding's desk he decreed that no one should leave on her, which would take it until mid-October at the earliest. Dejectedly, I went along to see my pals in the Movements Office to see what chance there might be of anything meanwhile. I was met with broad smiles. They had negotiated a deal with BOAC to take up any spare capacity on their flights passing through to Cairo. The first half dozen of us would fly from the airfield at Khormaksar tomorrow, so I had better get my kit packed. I went off in a daze, with visions of a comfortable seat and being waited on by a charming air hostess. I even stopped to wonder whether the lad in Masirah I had been sent to relieve over a year ago might be on the list. I hadn't got there and I knew that no one else had been chosen to take my place.

By plane to Cairo

The next morning we chosen few gathered at the airport with all our kit. Our 'luxury' aircraft turned out to be the civilian version of the Lockheed Hudson, a light aircraft used on reconnaissance and anti-submarine duties. Passengers sat on wooden benches around the inside of the fuselage with all the baggage and any freight stacked in the middle. No sign of any cabin crew or in-flight refreshments! At least it was more comfortable than my only previous flight, stowed away in the bowels of a Blenheim.

Our first stop was a RAF Staging Post on a tiny island in the middle of the Red Sea to refuel. The island seemed to be comprised of an earth landing strip, a small jetty and a few huts. The only human beings were the airstrip crew, one Corporal and two Airmen. Their uniform was boots, stockings, shorts and a very dark suntan! No doubt our flight was some sort of reciprocal arrangement for services rendered.

Eventually we reached Cairo in the late evening and were taken to a nearby transit camp. I would like to say we enjoyed a good night's sleep, but we were asked to provide a night patrol of the camp, which included a separate WAAF compound, presumably for girls working at Air Headquarters. As we were on our way again by dawn's early light, we didn't even have time to say "Hello".

A drive down the desert road in the inevitable 3-ton truck took us to Kasfareet for my third stay there. Mercifully, this time it was very brief. On booking in there I was asked the inevitable question: "Date of embarkation?" (from the UK)

"15th August 1941," said I.

"You mean 1942 don't you?"

"No – 1941," said I.

The clerk looked at me in amazement and asked. "Where the hell have you been then? We are sending home people with late 1942 dates at the moment!"

At least that meant I was on the very next draft.

With the war over and all the ocean-going troopships busily occupied in bringing troops home from India and the Far East, or cross-Atlantic trips, the journey home took a more interesting route. Stage one was from Port Said to Toulon in the South of France, thence by train to Dieppe and then a Cross Channel ferry to Newhaven.

Troopship to Marseilles

Our journey began early one morning by boarding a train bound for Port Said. Most of the route ran alongside the northern end of the Suez Canal, an area new to me, and busy with canal traffic. We arrived that afternoon and boarded the smallish troopship that would be our home for the next 10 days. It was French, elderly, slow and very basic indeed. We were to discover that once on the move it had the ability to pitch and roll at the same time, even in a calm sea. We had a moderately rough crossing, which, when accentuated by this strange trait, meant that all on our Mess except myself and one other lad suffered almost continual seasickness. Even when at anchor in Valetta harbour on a calm day you could detect this movement! I imagine its normal role in pre-war days was ferrying Foreign Legion troops between their base in Marseilles and Algiers in North Africa.

My suspicion that we were on a ship normally used for short-haul journeys only were heightened by the fact that it appeared to have no cooking facilities whatsoever. All we ever needed was a tin opener. We just collected our daily ration of tinned pilchards, sardines, corned beef and the like, together with a supply of hard tack (and 'hard' was the operative word: those ship's biscuits were like iron!) – hardly appetising food for the poor souls suffering from seasickness.

You can imagine the immense relief felt by all on board when eventually the French coast came in view early one morning. We docked, disembarked and were marched up to a tented transit camp on a racecourse.

Even though the war was over and secrecy was no longer paramount, information about our journey was often sparse. We were eventually told that we would be travelling by train to northern France. Protocol decreed that the Royal Navy, being the Senior Service, would leave on the first train that very night. Army lads would be on the second train the following night, while the junior Service, the RAF would bring up the rear on the third night. Meanwhile, we could enjoy the very limited resources available. On no account would we be able to leave camp. Having no francs, or even sterling to exchange, that was not a problem, and I doubt if anyone harboured ideas of deserting at that stage.

Actually, it was very pleasant and relaxing to enjoy the scenery and greenery after years of mainly desert or scrubland and twelve months of Aden's barrenness. I vowed to return one day, which I did many times in later years. All the cookhouse staff were French girls but, having seen many thousands of servicemen come and go, German during the war and many other nationalities afterwards, they showed not the slightest interest in us. Sad!

The evening of day three came and we were told to fill our water bottles and given our travel rations of two doorstep bully beef sandwiches. There would be meal stops en route and we were due to reach Dieppe the following afternoon. We were then marched off to a nearby station to await our train. I have been through that station many times since, with all the memories that brings, but the racecourse has long disappeared under industrial and housing development.

Slow Train to Dieppe

It was about 10pm before our train pulled in and we clambered aboard. The carriages had wooden slatted seats and the usual notices were all in German. The rumour was that their normal use was on suburban services in the Berlin area. Motive power was provided by an overhead electric engine. Even in those days, the development of the French railway system was well ahead of ours at home.

The train moved off. We ate our travel rations and fell asleep, probably dreaming of the breakfast that morning would bring. I awoke at daybreak to find us travelling at a good speed, somewhere in France. Later research with the aid of a map would place us nearing Carcassonne, as I remember seeing the medieval fortifications there. Shortly afterwards we pulled into another station, Castelnaudary, and stopped.

Was this our breakfast stop? Actually no, and we remained there, unmoving, until midday. I looked so long at the section of the station buildings opposite my window that when I travelled that way many years later I could identify it in an instant! A message was passed down the train that there had been a derailment ahead and we were being diverted.

As it was down a single-track non-electrified branch line, we were waiting for a sufficiently powerful steam locomotive to cope with our long train to be obtained.

At last we moved off, at a stately pace of 15 to 20 mph, down a very pretty rural line, eventually grinding to a halt alongside an apple orchard. Now sitting looking at trees laden with ripe fruit was just too tempting for some, and they began to climb down and head for those rosy red apples! This galvanised our Military Police escort, who rounded them up, got them back on board and locked all the carriage doors for the rest of the journey.

Eventually the cause of our delay appeared, a train heading in the other direction, passing us in the crossing loop. Off we went again at last, and were soon into the station at Castres. Even if we had not been locked in there would have been no point trying to obtain something to eat, as we had been warned not to, the French being in such dire straits and themselves on minimal rations.

Some time later we moved off again, heading north, to pick up the main line again at Cahors. It was a lovely evening and the countryside was so beautiful. Even then, 4 months after the war had ended, German Prisoners of War were being moved south. At least two trainloads passed us that evening. They were not enjoying the comparative comfort of our wooden seated carriages, but were travelling in goods vans with open doors. Ironically, we were locked in on our train and they were not! The majority of them seemed to be young lads of 15 to 16 years of age.

Darkness fell and we rumbled on. Hungry though we were by then, most of us dozed off to sleep for our second night on the train. Later on, around midnight, I think on the outskirts of Limoges, we stopped again. We heard the voices of members of our escort walking around alongside the track. Eventually we learnt that it was one of our feeding places, but being so late all the staff had long gone home. We should be getting a meal at the next one, on the outskirts of Paris.

Come the dawn we were much further north. From here on, right through to the coast, we slowed to cross every railway bridge at a crawl. Without exception they were all temporary wooden structures, replacing bridges that had been destroyed in the run up to D-Day, either by air strikes, sabotage by the French Resistance or, if any remained, by the retreating Germans.

Circling Paris

As we negotiated our way from south to north through the Parisian rail system, it was noticeable that every former marshalling yard was reduced to a vast open space with just the two running lines passing through the middle. No doubt all the rails had long since been converted into guns and tanks and the wooden sleepers used for fuel. Many years later, when I visited the room in a corner of a Technical College in Rheims, where the eventual ceasefire was signed, I saw a huge wall map of France, showing the running state and availability of every line in the country on 8th May 1945, which brought everything back to mind. The room had been part of General Eisenhower's headquarters during the latter stages of the war. Although he had not been present to sign the document himself, his deputy, Air Chief Marshall Tedder, had done so on his behalf, and I had the opportunity to sit in his chair at his position at the table on that day.

We completed our circuit of Paris, joined the mainline running north and quite quickly came to our meal stop. Needless to say, we were more than ready for our breakfast! Nothing happened for a while and then the message came. They could not feed us as they were already dealing with a trainload of troops heading in the opposite direction. We would be fed when we reached Dieppe.

Off we went again and at Rouen turned off on the line running down to Dieppe, a very pretty route along the bottom of a peaceful, wooded valley, although judging by the number of crashed German, British and American aircraft to be seen, it had been far from peaceful during the war.

At last we reached Dieppe, the carriage doors were unlocked, we disembarked with all our kit and there was a hot meal ready and waiting for us, our first for 48 hours.

Ferry to Newhaven

Once fed and watered, we were marched the short distance to the docks, where a Southern Railways Cross-Channel ferry, the SS *Canterbury*, was waiting for us. The ferries in those days were not like the giant car ferries of today, so most of us finished up standing on the open deck with our kit, packed like proverbial sardines. At least we could see where we were going.

A final scare

At last we set sail on a calm and pleasant late afternoon crossing to Newhaven. About half way across we could clearly see the English shore when, without any warning, we turned sharply through 90 degrees, so sharply, in fact, that we were all thrown against each other. Those of us near enough to the ships' side saw the reason why. Bobbing along very close to us was an evil-looking mine, one of those with detonators poking out all around it like porcupine quills that we have all seen illustrations of in books but never wished to see in real life. There were some Navy lads on board with rifles, who managed to explode it and remove the danger for other shipping. I dread to think what might have happened if we had been making the crossing after dark. What a tragedy it would have been for many of us who had been abroad for years and survived so much hardship and danger, to lose our lives in that manner within sight of our homeland.

England at last

I am sure that we all gave a great sigh of relief when we finally moored up alongside at Newhaven. I know I did! As soon as the gangplank was in position, we began to disembark in single file, kitbags on shoulders, straight across the quay and through Customs. This was in the days before the advent of Red and Green channels, when everyone would be asked if they had anything to declare. To give the Customs Officers their due, they simply stood in a line along one side of the Customs hall and let us pass by in complete silence. I wonder how many tens of thousands of service personnel they had greeted in that fashion?

Through Customs and on to the Station Platform, where a long train awaited us, engine simmering gently at its head. I spotted a LMS carriage, way up the platform and, knowing from experience that they were by far the most comfortable of any of the four mainline companies, I made straight for it, slung my kitbag on the rack and took a corner seat, where I could see where our route would take us. What bliss to sit back in an upholstered seat for the first time in over four years! I luxuriated in the sensation while the train filled up, and determined to stay awake all night if necessary.

Some time later, the Guard blew his whistle and gave the "right away". The driver gave his answering toot and we moved off. I remember hearing the sound of the engine passing under a road bridge as we accelerated away. The next thing I knew, dawn had broken and I had no idea where we were or how we had got there. The unaccustomed comfort had been too much for me.

Dispersal Camp

Wherever we were, we were in a built up area and travelling eastwards. Soon afterwards we arrived at Upminster and we were transferred to our Dispersal camp. Here efficiency reigned supreme. We were immediately confronted by a full English breakfast, the likes of which we had not seen for many a year, not to mention charming girls who could speak English! So unused were we to the size of the helpings, that many of us were struggling to get it all down. Most of us were equally unused to the company of girls, English-speaking or otherwise.

Next came the necessary paperwork but first a full medical. I weighed in at just over seven stone, compared with my normal 11 stone or thereabouts. There was our tropical kit to dispose of, and chance to replace any other items as necessary. Then came the really important things we had all been waiting for; 28-day disembarkation leave passes, ration cards and a railway warrant to our home station. By late afternoon it was all done and dusted and we were free to go.

That all fitted in very well for me, as my mother was in the London area, so I was able to give her a surprise call. No phones, mobiles or otherwise, in those days, though we were allowed one free telegram, which I used to forewarn my Gran in Shaldon of my imminent arrival.

By train to Devon and home

The next day it was off to Paddington to catch the 9am train. It was a wonderful feeling, which got better and better all the way. Emerging from Whiteball tunnel and knowing that I was in Devon, the familiar sounds and sights of Exeter St Davids station, rumbling off over the River Exe on the last lap, down the Exe estuary, past Dawlish Warren and along the sea wall past Dawlish, out of Smugglers Tunnel to see the sweep of coastline as far as Berry Head and then into Teignmouth Station. Even now when I come down that line, the memories come flooding back.

On leaving the train, I slung my kitbag on my shoulder and made for the exit, prepared for the walk home. There had been so little time or opportunity to warn anyone that I was not expecting to be met.

My girlfriend Miriam, who had written to me every week that I was away, without fail, had been directed into war work, the female equivalent of conscription, well over a year ago, soon after her 18th birthday, and was in Gloucestershire. But as I came out of the station, there she was! Her unforgettable first words to me were to say how brown I was! Well, after all those years I certainly had a suntan, but was so used to it I had almost forgotten what it was like to be otherwise.

A modern-day view of Shaldon.

The amazing thing was that we walked off up the road side by side, chatting away as if it was only a few weeks since we last met, rather than well over four years, when she was but 15. What a truly wonderful feeling it was, the war over, hopefully years of peace stretching ahead and four weeks in which to share and enjoy each other's company – and, for me, to adjust to a more normal lifestyle.

We soon came to the approach road to Shaldon Bridge. It was a beautiful sunny day with a few cotton-wool clouds. The tide was in and the estuary full of water, sparkling in the sunshine. To the west, Dartmoor filled the horizon in all its majesty and across the bridge was my beloved Shaldon.

I WAS HOME AT LAST!

~ End ~

Epilogue

I was promoted to Sergeant as from the day I stepped ashore at Newhaven. Then followed postings to RAF Broadwell, 51 Group HQ Bushy Hall Watford, RAF Defford and RAF Chivenor on routine type duties.

Someone, somewhere then decided that I should be a Trade Instructor. Two years of coping with a class of 40 18 year old National Service Lads for five and a half days a week from the morning parade to the end of the day "Dismiss", not to mention barrack inspections, kit inspections and all the other joys of daily RAF life. What a baptism of fire that was!

Then followed almost two years at my old Apprentice Training School then at RAF St Athan. My final year was spent teaching RAF Law and Administration at the Middle East NCO Training school at RAF Shallufa in the Suez Canal Zone and then at RAF Nicosia in Cyprus when it moved there. The training and personnel development skills I acquired stood me in good stead in civilian life.

My RAF career ended in June 1953, four months having been added due to the Korean War. I obtained work with W H Cullen, multiple grocers. In 1955 I took the first year Institute of Certificated Grocers Exams, obtaining the top mark in the country. Later that year a career change took me to the Export Department of Philips Electrical Ltd until 1966. I then joined the recently formed Construction Industry Training Board as a Supervisor, retiring in 1986 as a Senior Manager.

THE AUTHOR, WITH SERVICE MEDALS, 2012.